Quick & Clever Cross Stitch

MERRY
Christmas
PEACE AND JOY TO ALL
abcdefghijklm
nopqrstuvwx
yz123456
O LITTLE TOWN
OF BETHLEHEM

Quick & Clever Cross Stitch

Helen Philipps

A DAVID & CHARLES BOOK

David & Charles is an F+W Publications Inc. company
4700 East Galbraith Road
Cincinnati, OH 45236

First published in the UK in 2006

A catalogue record for this book is available from the British Library.

ISBN-13: 978-0-7153-2174-4 hardback
ISBN-10: 0-7153-2174-9 hardback

ISBN-13: 978-0-7153-2478-3 paperback (USA only)
ISBN-10: 0-7153-2478-0 paperback (USA only)

Printed in China by SNP leefing
for David & Charles
Brunel House Newton Abbot Devon

Executive Editor Cheryl Brown
Editor Jennifer Proverbs
Art Editor Prudence Rogers
Production Controller Ros Napper
Project editor and chart preparation Lin Clements
Photographers Kim Sayer and Karl Adamson

Visit our website at www.davidandcharles.co.uk

David & Charles books are available from all good bookshops; alternatively you can contact our Orderline on 0870 9908222 or write to us at FREEPOST EX2 110, D&C Direct, Newton Abbot, TQ12 4ZZ (no stamp required UK mainland); US customers call 800-289-0963 and Canadian customers call 800-840-5220.

(Picture, page 1): This beautiful Christmas sampler shows what you will be able to achieve using the ideas in this book. It uses Sampler Template 7, the same one as the Family Sampler on page 29. It is the most ambitious template in this book and gives lots of scope for working on a theme and including a large variety of motifs. Christmas has many colourful festive images so it was great fun choosing which ones to include here. You will find the angels, the Bethlehem scene and all the festive motifs in the seasons section of the Motif Library on pages 78–88. There are plenty of others to pick from, so choose your own favourites.

Contents

Wedding Day
CATHERINE
ANDREW
12 JUNE 2006
To Love and to Cherish

Spring
summer
AUTUMN
WINTER

Welcome to our Patch

Introduction

Samplers are a delightful way to use simple cross stitch and backstitch to create a small piece of art. They make wonderful gifts: they can be stitched to record information, to commemorate special occasions and to celebrate unique events and achievements in our lives. Individual motifs from a sampler can also be used to create a whole range of smaller gifts and keepsakes.

This book has been designed to be as versatile as possible to enable you not only to stitch the attractive samplers provided throughout the book but also to create your own one-of-a-kind samplers by using the eight highly versatile sampler templates provided on pages 92–100. All of the charts are produced at the same scale so it is easy to pick and mix motifs from the eight samplers charted and the huge library of motifs on pages 38–91.

There are four ways you can use this book to create memorable embroideries:

1 You can work the eight 'stitch-off-the-page' samplers exactly as they are, as charming projects in their own right.

2 You can use the eight templates and the Motif Library to stitch alternate motifs and create highly individual samplers.

3 You can adapt the eight sampler templates even further, changing their overall design completely, moving sections around to create your own totally unique and personal samplers.

4 You can use the huge selection of designs in the Motif Library for quick-stitch projects, such as cards, trinket pots, book covers, coasters, plant pokes and other accessories.

1 Working the Stitch-off-the-Page Samplers

Eight complete samplers have been provided for those of you who want to get stitching right away. These delightful samplers reflect the most popular subjects in our lives, including anniversaries, home and family, Christmas and memorable events.

Each sampler is based on a sampler template – a cross-stitched framework, within which the various motifs and lettering are stitched. Work the stitch-off-the-page samplers by following the instructions and chart given with each project. You could also replace some motifs to personalize the embroidery. Look out for the 'Pick 'n' Mix' ideas throughout the book.

Using Chart Keys

Each stitch-off-the-page sampler (pages 8–37) has its own chart key that should be used only when stitching that particular sampler, including all the motifs already charted within its framework.

If substituting a motif already charted on your chosen sampler with one from the Motif Library (pages 38–91), always stitch that particular motif using the key provided on the library page where it is charted (occasionally one key is given for two pages that appear side by side). This will ensure the correct colours for each individual motif are used.

2 Using the Sampler Templates

Eight different sampler layouts have been designed as basic templates with sections that can be filled with motifs and lettering of your choice (see pages 92–100 for the eight templates). The idea is to use a template as a starting point and fill each section by selecting from the hundreds of motifs and borders in the Motif Library covering the family, home, leisure, work and the seasons. The library also has sayings and alphabets to help you personalize your work and make it easy to create a special sampler, reflecting yourself, your life, your family, friends, hobbies and interests.

1 Choose a sampler template and photocopy it. Decide what theme you would like your sampler to have and then choose the motifs from the Motif Library and the other charts in this book.

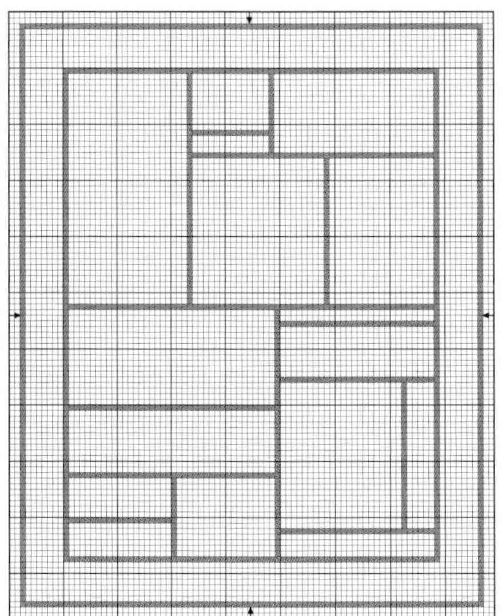

Using Sampler Template 6 as your starting point you can select motifs and lettering to fill the boxes and produce a sampler plan – like this sports sampler idea. Make a note where each motif came from so you can follow the correct chart key. Page 25 shows this template being used as a colourful Christmas Sampler.

Using Motifs

2 Check the motifs you want to use will fit the spaces available on your sampler template (see overleaf for Will It Fit?). Photocopy the motifs, cut them out around the edges and use a temporary spray adhesive to position them on your sampler template – this will allow you to re-position motifs if necessary. (Don't worry if the darker template lines don't match up.) Alternatively, use a pen to copy the outline of the motif on to the sampler plan to check it fits the space. You can also adapt the motifs in this book, particularly the people motifs – see Adapting People, below. You may also want to create a mirror image of a motif – see overleaf.

Adding Words

3 Decide what names, dates and other words or sayings you want to use in your sampler. You will find some events, sayings and greetings charted in the Motif Library but you can easily create your own by using the charted alphabets on pages 90–91. Using a sharp pencil, work out the lettering on squared paper, remembering to allow for the spaces between letters and words. Work out the size of the space where you want to position the lettering by counting the squares across and down in that space on your sampler plan. Position the lettering centrally, adjusting the spaces in between if necessary so that it's even.

4 Assess the final layout of your sampler; if there are gaps you can fill them with tiny motifs, e.g., hearts, flowers, bees and butterflies. When your chart is complete, count the total number of stitches across the height, and then the width. This is the stitch count of your complete design, which you will need to know to calculate how much fabric you need – see Calculating Design Size, overleaf. Mark the chart centre so you know where to begin stitching.

5 Choose your fabric colour to complement the type of sampler you wish to create, and make sure you leave plenty of room around the outside for framing. Choose your thread colours; those used in this book are DMC stranded cotton (floss) but you could use other thread ranges (ask at your local needlecraft store for conversion charts). Choose a blunt-ended tapestry needle, size 26 should be fine, and you are ready to begin stitching!

Adapting People

The figures in the family motif pages can be used to represent people in your sampler. If you wish to make them more like someone you know, you can change details on your motif by altering hair colour and adding clothes they might wear. You can also add spectacles or other distinguishing details to make the person more recognizable. See how the man here can be changed into a cricketer.

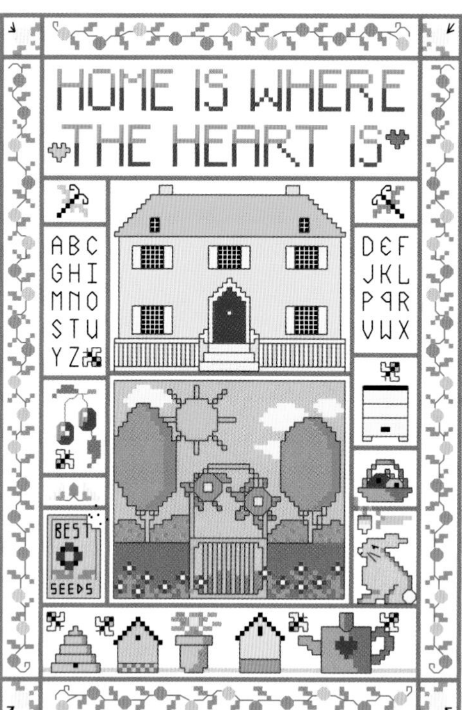

This bright sampler shows how a sampler template is used to feature different motifs. It uses Template 5 (the same one as the wedding sampler on page 23). The house, garden gate picture, all the colourful motifs and border can be found in the home section of the Motif Library (pages 50–59). Choose other motifs on a garden theme if you wish. This sampler also uses bee charms to add to the garden effect, or you could stitch extra bees and butterflies from the charted motifs.

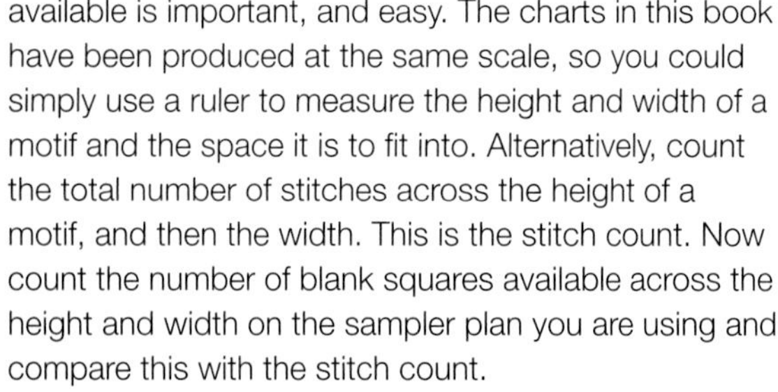

Will It Fit?

Determining whether a motif will fit in the space available is important, and easy. The charts in this book have been produced at the same scale, so you could simply use a ruler to measure the height and width of a motif and the space it is to fit into. Alternatively, count the total number of stitches across the height of a motif, and then the width. This is the stitch count. Now count the number of blank squares available across the height and width on the sampler plan you are using and compare this with the stitch count.

Once you know that the motif fits the space, find the centre of the motif and centre of the space and begin stitching outwards from there, to ensure the motif will fit centrally into the space. Most motifs look better with a few squares of unworked fabric around them but sometimes it looks good breaking over the edge of a sampler plan box, adding liveliness to your design, like the cat's tail, above.

Calculating Design Size

The charts and motifs in this book were designed to fit 14-count Aida or 28-count linen or evenweave fabric. You can stitch the designs on fabric with a lower or higher count but it will change the overall size. Being able to calculate the eventual size of a sampler design means you can decide how much fabric you need for a project or whether a design will fit a specific picture frame. Always add a generous margin when calculating fabric requirements, to allow for finishing and making up – 13cm (5in) to both dimensions when stitching a sampler.

Calculate design size as follows: count the number of stitches in each direction on the chart (or motif) and then divide by the stitch count of the embroidery fabric you want to use.

For example, a design on 14-count Aida of 140 stitches x 140 ÷ 14 = a finished design size of 10 x 10in (25 x 25cm). The same design worked on finer 16-count Aida would have a smaller finished size of 8¾ x 8¾in (22 x 22cm). When calculating design sizes for evenweave fabrics, divide the fabric count by 2 before you start, because evenweave is worked over two threads not one block as with Aida fabric.

Creating Mirror Images

Using motifs as mirror images can be very effective and create an attractive symmetry to a design. Some of the images in the charted stitch-off-the-page samplers and in the Motif Library have been produced as mirror images but you can easily do this yourself. Simply trace the motif, flip the tracing over and copy the design on to squared graph paper (some is supplied at the end of the book) and colour in the design with pencils or felt-tipped pens. Alternatively, scan the motif into a computer and reflect the image.

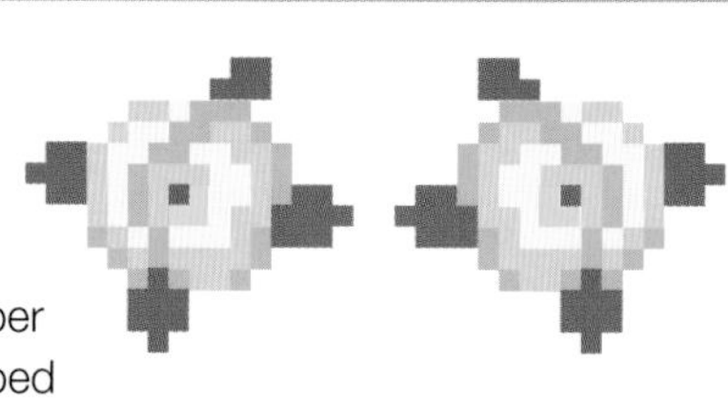

3 Adapting the Sampler Templates

The sampler templates are also the perfect starting point to inspire you to design your own totally unique samplers to celebrate occasions and anniversaries special to you. You will find that the templates are highly versatile, as the two family sampler plans below show. Instead of using a plan as it appears on the page, take the parts of it that appeal to you, adapting the shape and even mixing it with a part of another plan.

The sampler plan above is a smaller version of the stitch-off-the-page Happy Families sampler (page 29). Here, the names, house and pets section has been removed, and the saying and border moved up. You could use other combinations of sections. For example, omit the alphabet and keep the family, names, house and pets. To change people to represent your own family, look in the family section of the Motif Library and also Adapting People page 5.

1 Choose a sampler template you would like to use (see pages 92–100) and photocopy it (or copy on to graph paper). Cut out the parts you want to use and reassemble the plan the way you want it. Decide on a theme or subject and choose motifs from the Motif Library and other charts in this book.

2 Now follow steps 2–5 from Using the Sampler Templates on page 5 to create your own unique embroidery.

This very small version of the main Family Sampler is quick to stitch but still makes a charming family keepsake.

Charting Your Own Motifs

Although there are a huge number of motifs in this book, you may wish to include something extra. To chart a special motif of your own you can use any clear picture or photo (e.g., of your own home or cat or dog). If it's too large make a smaller copy. Place a piece of tracing paper over the design and trace it carefully. Transfer it on to squared paper. Square up the traced image, removing details too small to stitch. Colour in the motif with pencils or felt pens. Cut out the motif and add it to your master sheet.

4 Using the Motif Library for Small Projects

The wonderful selection of delightful motifs in the Motif Library will ensure you never run out of ideas for small quick-stitch gifts and mementoes.

Each of the eight stitch-off-the-page sampler chapters feature an idea for a smaller project, such as a gift tag, key ring and greetings cards. There are many companies providing ready-made items for embroidery (see Suppliers page 104) and look in your local craft store for ideas.

Choose a motif from the Library and check its finished size will fit your mount – see Calculating Design Size, opposite. Stitch the motif according to its chart key, using two strands of stranded cotton (floss) for cross stitch and one strand for backstitch and French knots. Mount your finished embroidery – the Making Up section on pages 101–103 describes how to mount work in ready-made items, in cards and in picture frames.

Happy Anniversary

This sampler uses Template 1, the nine patch design (page 92), and makes the perfect anniversary keepsake. It is filled with motifs of romance and good luck, and you can make it unique by personalizing it with the couple's names and anniversary date around the outside. The motifs in each square make charming gifts and tags and are very quick to stitch. Use this versatile template to create your own nine patch sampler on celebratory themes – two examples are shown on page 11.

Stitch count 83 x 83 Design size 15 x 15cm (6 x 6in)

You will need

- 30 x 30cm (12 x 12in) 28-count linen or 14-count Aida in pastel pink
- DMC stranded cotton (floss) as in the chart key
- Size 26 tapestry needle

1 Bind the edges of your fabric with masking tape or oversew to prevent fraying. Fold the fabric into quarters to find the centre and begin stitching here from the centre of the chart overleaf.

2 Work out the names and date for your sampler on squared paper using a pencil and eraser, using the alphabet and numbers charts on pages 90–91. Stitch the anniversary year in the central heart, and the anniversary details around the outside (see Adding Words, page 5).

3 Work over two threads of linen or one block of Aida, using two strands of cotton (floss) for cross stitch and one for French knots and backstitching.

4 When all stitching is complete, press your work carefully and frame as a picture (see page 102 for advice).

Rose gift tag

This sweet little gift tag is simplicity itself to stitch. If you prefer you could use any of the motifs from the main chart. Worked on white 14-count Aida, the embroidery is mounted into a ready-made tag. You could also work a small design like this as a key ring.

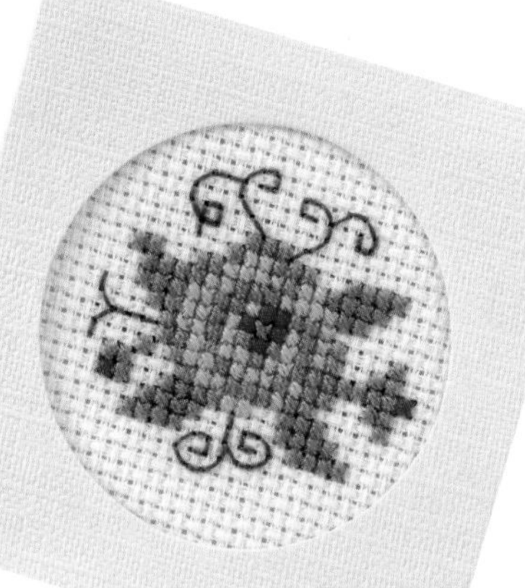

Pick 'n' Mix

Instead of repeating the dove, rose and bell motifs, adapt this anniversary sampler by choosing three other motifs – perhaps the pair of doves and the checked heart from page 42 of the Motif Library. See page 6 for Will It Fit? and Creating Mirror Images.

ALEXANDER AND MEGAN
THE ANNIVERSARY OF
11 JULY 2006
TO CELEBRATE
25

On Your
Wedding
Anniversary

On Your Anniversary

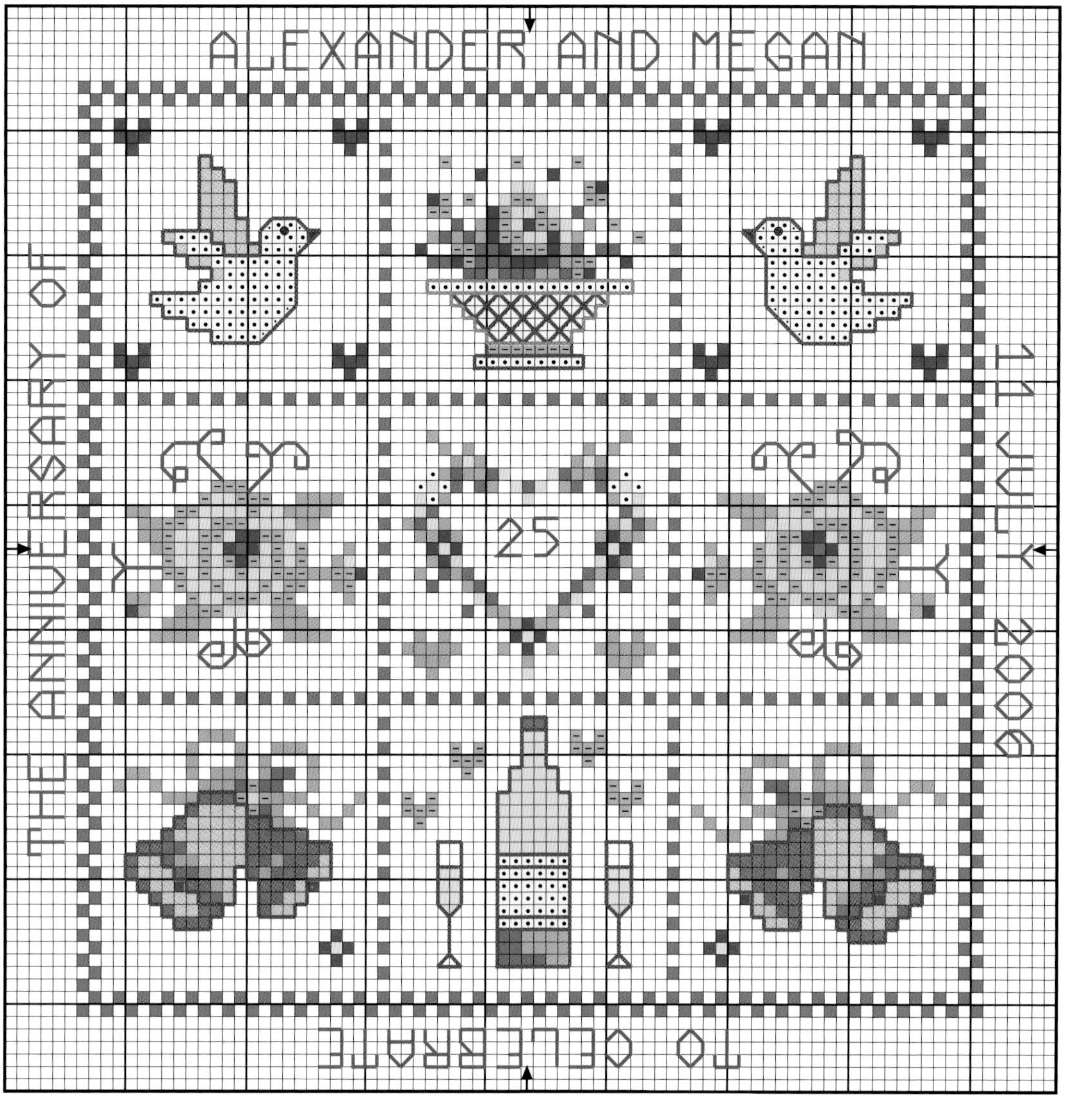

Happy Anniversary
DMC stranded cotton
Cross stitch

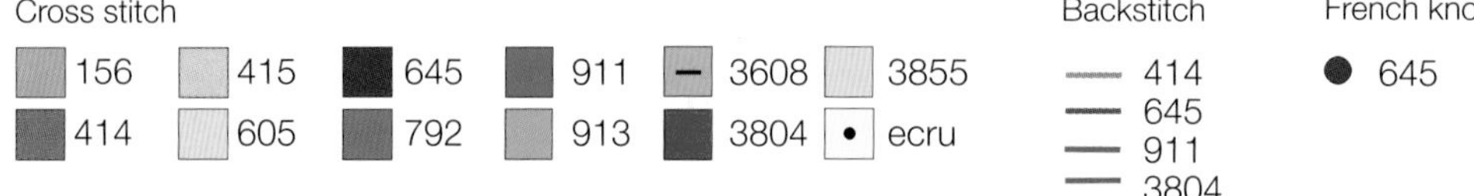

Pick 'n' Mix

You could replace the anniversary number in the central heart with the couple's initials, using the alphabets on pages 90 and 91. The sampler could also have a border added around the edge – see page 89 for ideas.

Celebrate Life

As you can see by these charming samplers, Sampler Template 1 is very simple to work and an extremely versatile plan. You can use nine separate images or mirror some to create a more symmetrical design. The sampler plans below show the layout of the various motifs.

Baby Nine Patch

This gorgeous sampler in pastel shades is suitable for either a boy or girl. All the motifs for this design can be found in the family section of the Motif Library, with simple flowers, flowerheads, stars and hearts scattered around the main motifs to add to the sampler's charm. The alphabet for this sampler is on page 90 and you can easily adapt the name and date – see Adding Words, page 5. Because the nine patch plan is so flexible, you can vary the design by rearranging the motifs or reflect any celebration you choose or selecting other motifs from the Motif Library.

Wedding Nine Patch

This pretty wedding sampler is easy to stitch using the simple nine patch from Sampler Template 1. You will find all the motifs in the family section of the Motif Library. Some of the motifs, such as the champagne bottle and glasses, have been stitched as mirror images, which can be very effective – see page 6 for how to do this. The alphabet and numbers chart is on page 90 and instructions for stitching the name and date for this sampler are on page 5. You could use different motifs, for example, add a church or flower bouquet in the central square instead of the heart and initials.

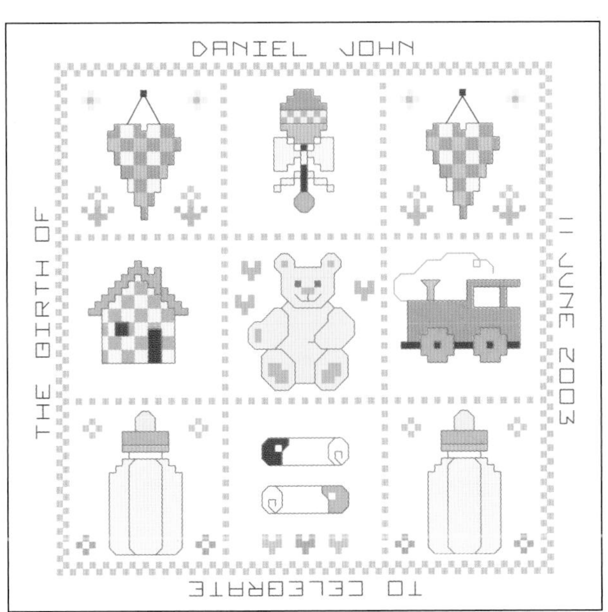

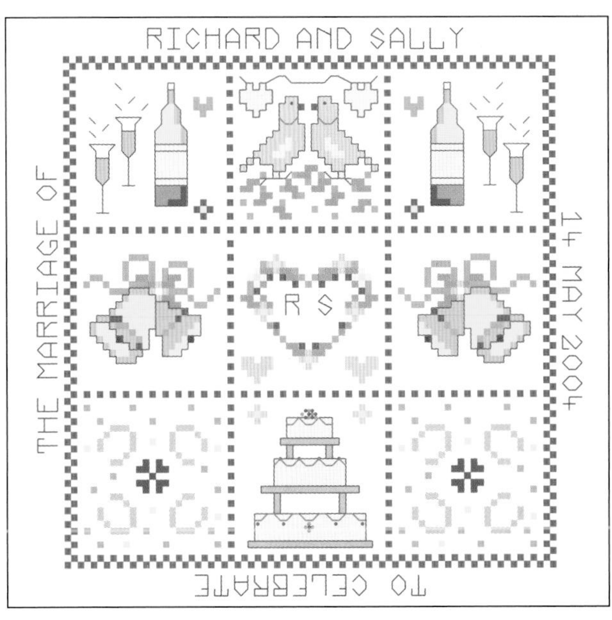

The Four Seasons

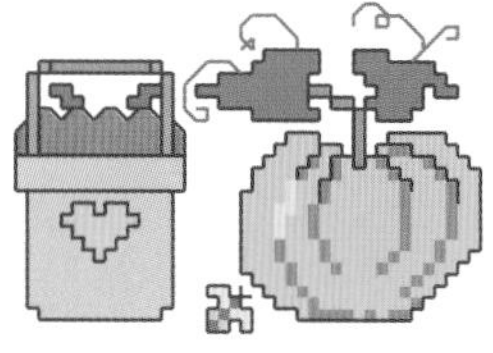

This charming sampler celebrates the four seasons using Sampler Template 2 (page 93). This is a simple and versatile plan with each of the four blocks interspersed with a small decorative floral band. In my sampler each block shows a different season, with birdhouses and flowers for spring, a sunny sandcastle picture for summer, a fat pumpkin and overflowing bucket of berries for autumn and two jolly snowmen with a berry-covered fir tree for winter. You might choose to work different sets of motifs in the template: for the keen gardener what about showing their productive garden – from packets of seeds, to fruits and vegetables growing, on to harvest time and then some delicious food?

Stitch count 165 x 43 Design size 30 x 8cm (11¾ x 3in)

You will need

- 46 x 25cm (18 x 10in) 14-count Aida or 28-count linen in white
- DMC stranded cotton (floss) as in the chart key
- Size 26 tapestry needle

1 Bind the edges of your fabric with masking tape or oversew to prevent fraying. Fold the fabric into quarters to find the centre and begin stitching here from the centre of the chart overleaf. The chart is split into two parts: if you wish, you could photocopy both parts and tape them together.

2 Work over one block of Aida or two threads of linen, using two strands of cotton (floss) for cross stitch and one for French knots and backstitching.

3 When all stitching is complete, press your work carefully and frame as a picture (see page 102 for advice).

Plant poke

Many parts of the Four Seasons sampler would make delightful greetings cards or small gifts, like this handy plant poke which features one of the birdhouses, plus a little bird button (Mill Hill, see Suppliers). Work the design of your choice on clear 14-count plastic canvas using six strands of thread for cross stitch and one for backstitch. Trim the design to within one row all round. Glue a garden stick to the back of the canvas and glue felt on to cover the back.

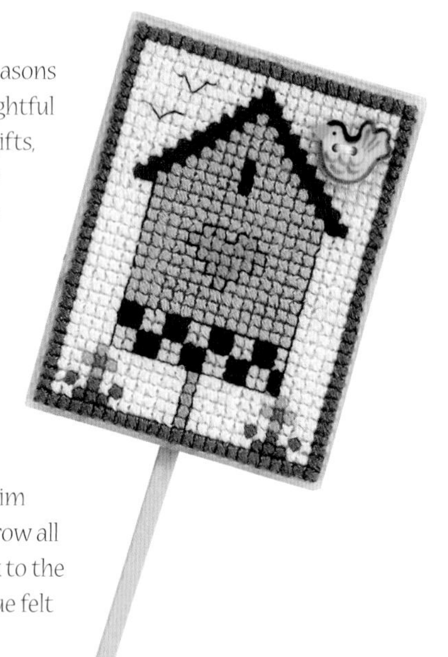

Pick 'n' Mix

You could change the flower border to a different one – what about the berry one on page 55 of the Motif Library or the heart border from page 80? The snowmen and tree at the bottom of the sampler could be replaced with a Christmas tree and presents from page 85. You could even include more seasonal motifs by widening Sampler Template 2. See page 6 for Will It Fit?

spring
SUMMER
AUTUMN
winter

TOP

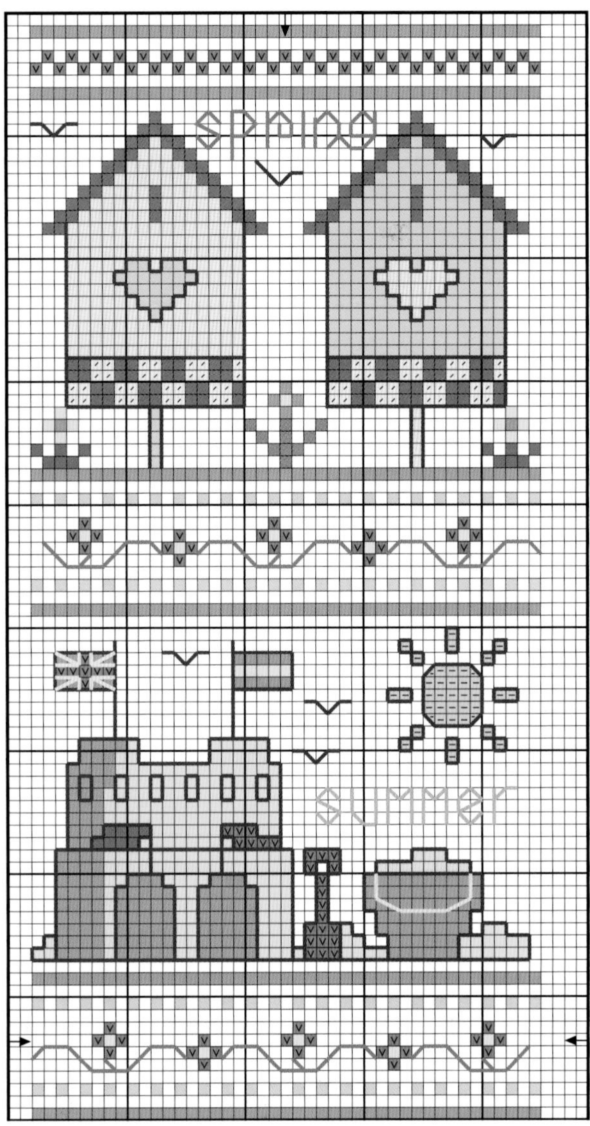

BOTTOM

← Join

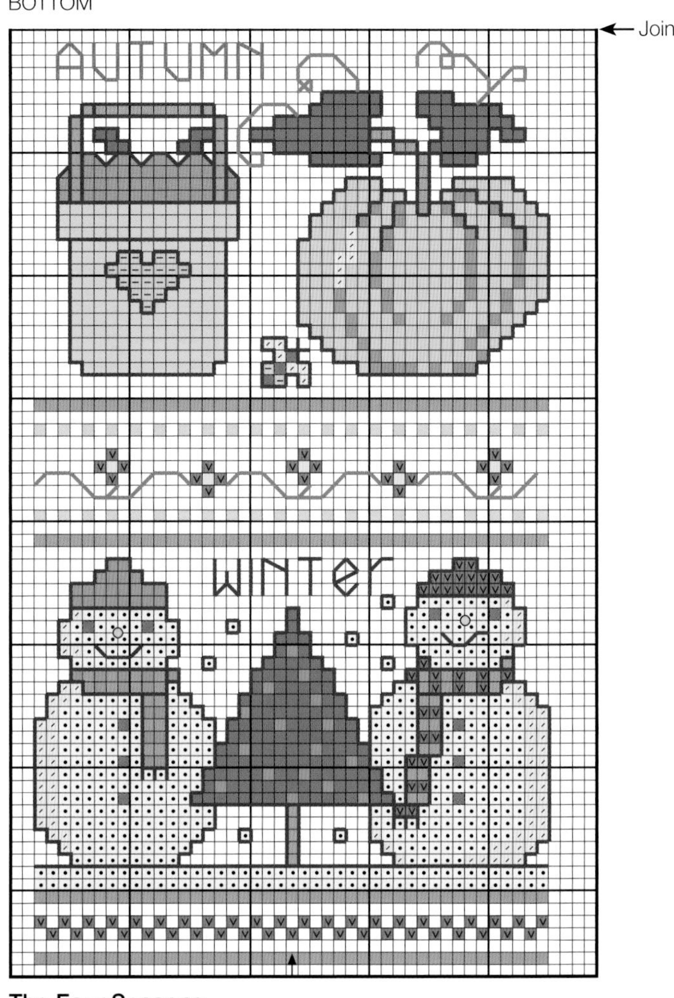

The Four Seasons
DMC stranded cotton

Cross stitch	Backstitch
153	334
318	413
334	562
356	963
402	48 variegated
413	
437	French knots
553	972
562	
725	
963	
964	
972	
3052	
ecru	
48 variegated	

Pick 'n' Mix

See what an individual effect you can create by changing the four seasonal motifs used in the sampler. Look through the Motif Library and the other samplers in the book for ideas. The bunny with spring flowers and butterflies from page 80 would work well for spring. Perhaps you could add a collection of smaller motifs to represent the seasons. See page 6 for Will It Fit?

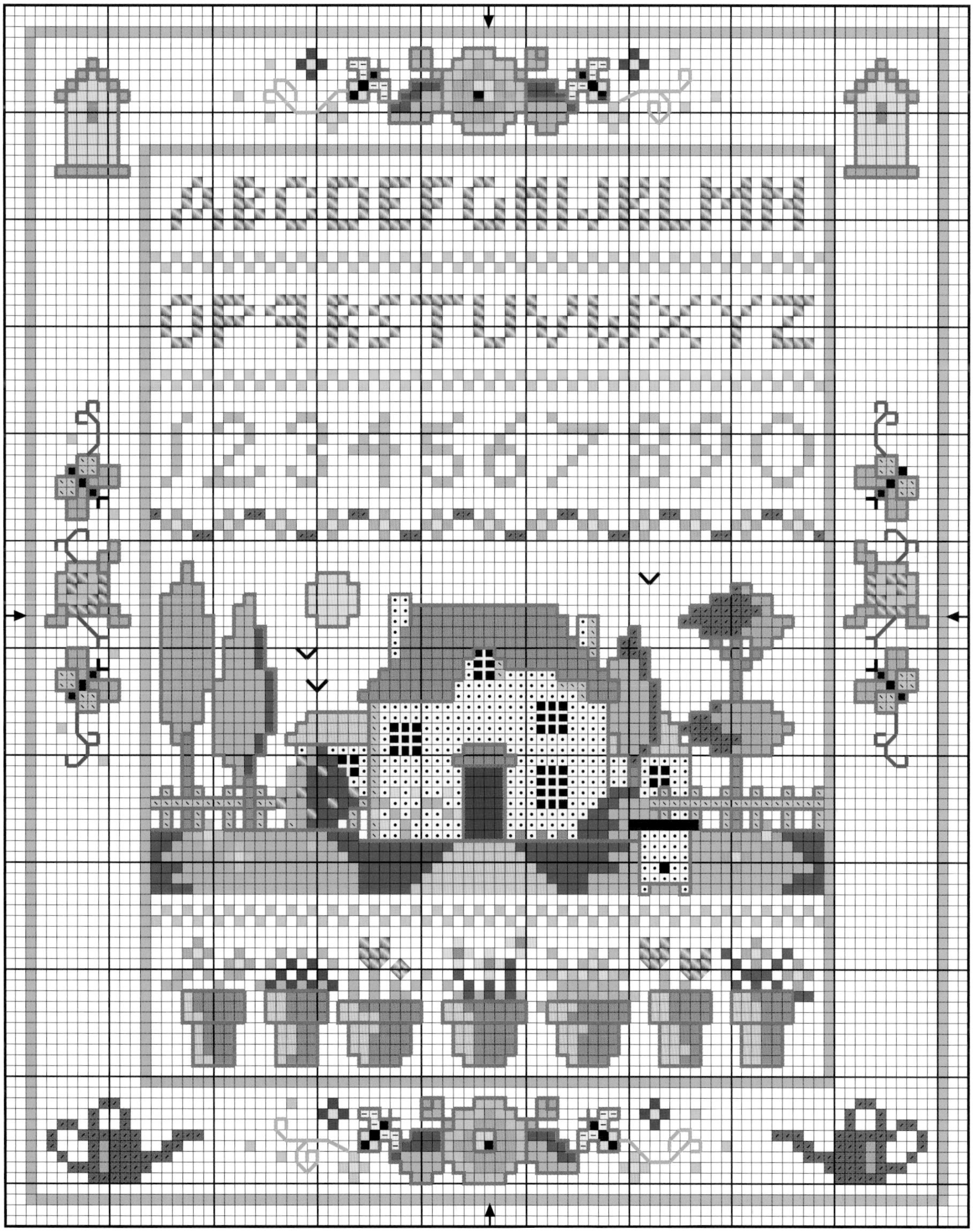

Home and Garden (instructions overleaf)
DMC stranded cotton
Cross stitch

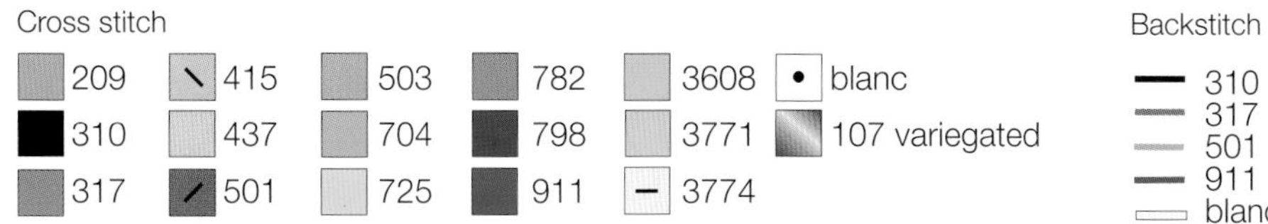

Home and Garden

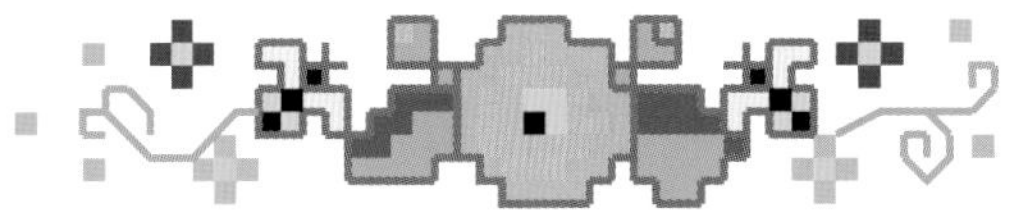

This design used Sampler Template 3, the traditional sampler shape (page 94) which was popular with early sampler makers. They frequently stitched a house and garden or large imaginary buildings with many windows to represent their school, together with an alphabet, a row of numbers, bands of pattern and an outer border. This design has a romantic cottage amid trees with a pretty flower garden and beehive and a border of flowers, bees and butterflies. There are optional bee and ladybird charms used on the sampler but you could add your favourite garden charms.

Stitch count 110 x 89 Design size 20 x 16cm (8 x 6¼in)

You will need

- 35 x 30cm (14 x 12in) 14-count Aida or 28-count linen in antique white
- DMC stranded cotton (floss) as in the chart key
- Size 26 tapestry needle
- Two bee and two ladybird charms (optional – see Suppliers)

1 Bind the edges of your fabric with masking tape or oversew to prevent fraying. Fold the fabric into quarters to find the centre and begin stitching here from the centre of the chart on the previous page.

2 Work over one block of Aida or two threads of linen, using two strands of cotton (floss) for cross stitch and one for backstitching and outlining. Sew on the charms with white cotton (floss) if you are using them.

3 When all stitching is complete, press your work carefully and frame as a picture (see page 102 for advice).

Key ring

This sweet little key ring is so simple to stitch and would make a charming gift. It is worked on white 14-count Aida. You could use any of the pots of flowers from the main sampler or perhaps one of the butterflies.

Pick 'n' Mix

To make this sampler more personal to you, try stitching a different house to represent your own (see Motif Library, page 50, 52 and 56). You could also choose small motifs from the library to replace the little charms, perhaps little insects. When using motifs from the library, remember to follow the relevant chart key there. See page 6 for Will It Fit?

ABCDEFGHIJKLMN
OPQRSTUVWXYZ
1234567890
please don't pick the flowers

Welcome Baby

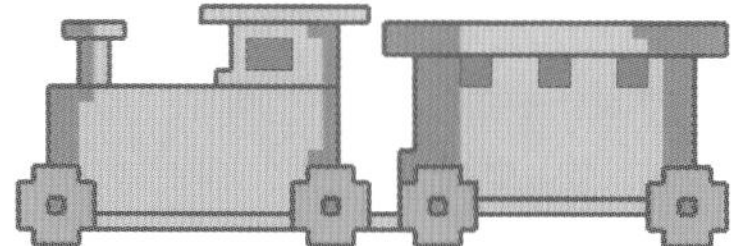

The bright colours and adorable motifs in this delightful sampler make it a perfect gift to commemorate the birth of a baby. It uses Sampler Template 4 (page 95) and shows how you can sometimes use motifs that break over the box they are in to add to the decorative effect. The name on the sampler is easily changed by using the alphabet and numbers charted on page 90.

Stitch count 134 x 95 Design size 24.5 x 17cm (9½ x 7in)

You will need

- 39 x 32cm (15 x 13in) 28-count linen or 14-count Aida in white
- DMC stranded cotton (floss) as in the chart key
- Size 26 tapestry needle

1 First work out the baby's name and birth date for your sampler on squared paper using a pencil and eraser (see page 5 for further advice).

2 Bind the edges of your fabric with masking tape or oversew to prevent fraying. Fold the fabric into quarters to find the centre and begin stitching here from the centre of the chart overleaf.

3 Work over two threads of linen or one block of Aida, using two strands of cotton (floss) for cross stitch and one for backstitching and outlining. Work the small stars in star stitch (see page 102) using one strand. Work the eyes in French knots in one strand.

4 When all stitching is complete, press your work carefully and frame as a picture (see page 102 for advice).

Baby card

Any of the motifs in the main design could be used for cards, like the cute rabbit shown here worked on white 14-count Aida and mounted in a cream card. You could also use the moon and stars and add the baby's name.

Pick 'n' Mix

Some of the motifs on the main sampler could be replaced with others from the Motif Library. Try stitching the pram from page 43 instead of the two yellow stars below the baby's name, or stitch the teddy bear and mice instead of the train. See page 6 for Will It Fit?

B A B Y
JESSICA ELIZABETH
MAY 14
2006
WISHING YOU THE MOON AND STARS

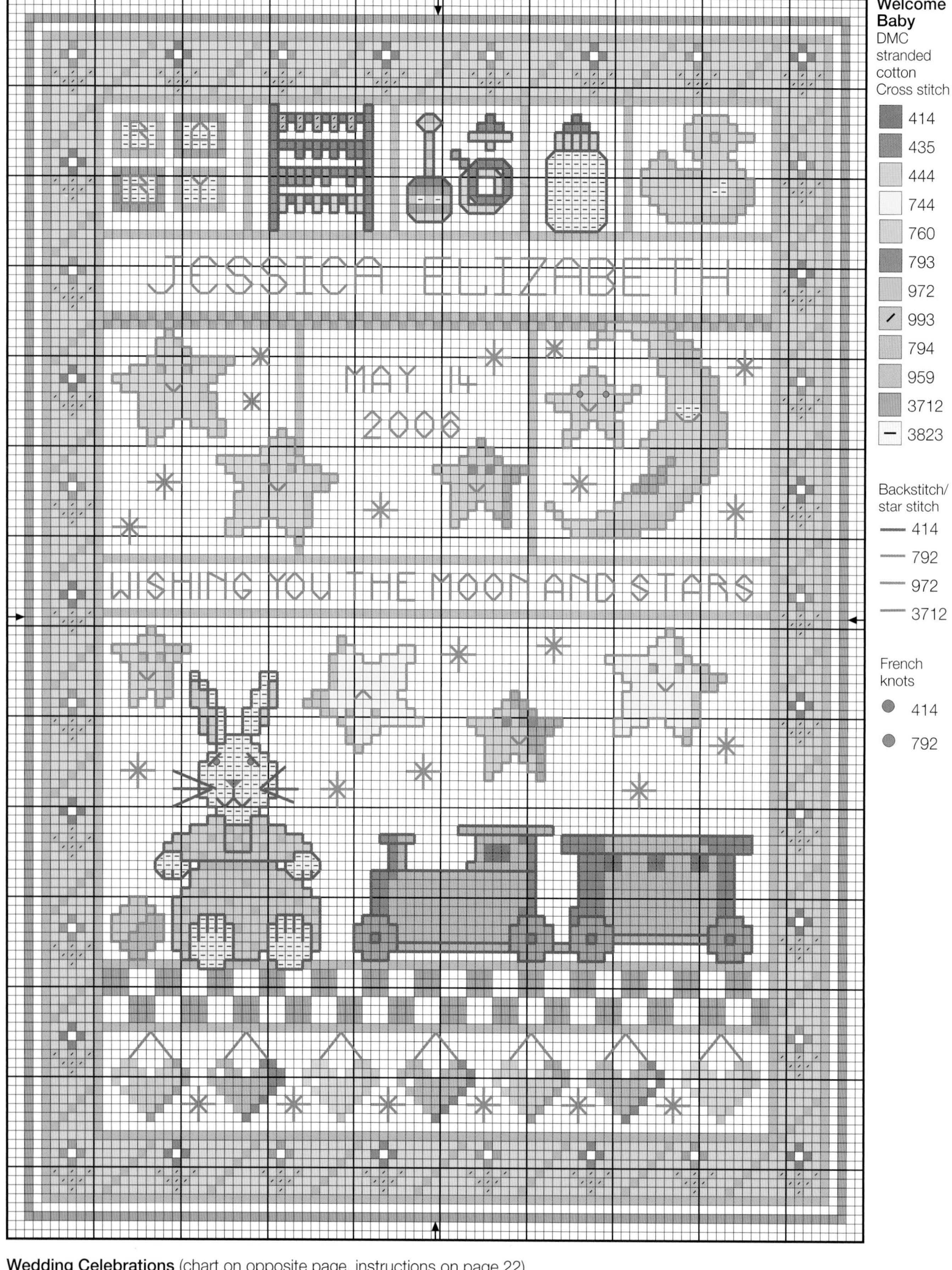

Wedding Celebrations (chart on opposite page, instructions on page 22)

DMC stranded cotton

Cross stitch

317	340	972	3689	3799	3823	125 light variegated	
318	415	3608	3746	3803	ecru	125 dark variegated	

Backstitch

317	3746
318	3803
972	125 light variegated

French knots

414

Wedding Day
CATHERINE
ANDREW
12 JUNE 2006
To Love and to Cherish

Wedding Celebrations

This delightful flowery design in pretty sugared-almond colours uses Sampler Template 5 (page 96), which is quite symmetrical and has plenty of boxes for individual wedding-theme motifs. It has curling honeysuckle, tiny blue forget-me-nots and roses in pink and red to symbolize lasting love. It is easy to personalize the sampler by using the alphabets and numbers on page 90.

Stitch count 153 x 103 Design size 28 x 19cm (11 x 7½in)

You will need

- 43 x 35cm (17 x 14in) 28-count linen or 14-count Aida in white
- DMC stranded cotton (floss) as in the chart key
- Size 26 tapestry needle

1 First work out the name and date for your sampler on squared paper using a pencil and eraser (see page 5 for further advice).

2 Bind the edges of your fabric with masking tape or oversew to prevent fraying. Fold the fabric into quarters to find the centre and begin stitching here from the centre of the chart on the previous page.

3 Work over two threads of linen or one block of Aida, using two strands of cotton (floss) for cross stitch and one for backstitching and outlining. Work French knots in one strand.

4 When all stitching is complete, press your work carefully and frame as a picture (see page 102 for advice).

Ring pillow

Part of the wedding sampler design has been used to create this matching ring pillow, worked over two threads of a white 28-count linen (or 14-count Aida if you prefer). The complete design is charted on page 49 of the Motif Library. See page 103 for making up the pillow. You could use the bride and groom motif to make a matching wedding card, while the smaller motifs are ideal for gift tags to make a present extra special.

Pick 'n' Mix

Use the alphabets charted on page 90 and 91 to create a message of your own at the base of the wedding sampler. You could also replace one of the topiary pots with the two Champagne glasses from page 42. You may want to use some motifs as mirror images – if so, see page 6 for Creating Mirror Images and Will It Fit?

Wedding Day
CATHERINE
ANDREW
12 JUNE 2006
To Love and to Cherish

Very Merry Christmas

This sampler uses Sampler Template 6 (page 97) and is perfect to stitch a collection of small Christmas motifs. This sweet design features plenty of Christmas images, like Santa, a tall Christmas tree, a knitted Christmas stocking, a little white church and a snowy scene. I stitched it on raw linen to give it a rustic, folk-art appearance but it would also look effective on other colours, such as cream or navy blue. It would be easy to change the words around the outside of the sampler to your own greeting, using the alphabet on page 90 – see page 5 for further advice. Another Christmas sampler using template 8 is shown on page 1.

Stitch count 104 x 85   Design size 19 x 15.5cm (7½ x 6in)

You will need

- 34 x 30cm (13 x 12in) 28-count raw linen or 14-count Rustico Aida
- DMC stranded cotton (floss) as in the chart key
- Size 26 tapestry needle
- White star button (optional – see Gregory Knopp, Suppliers)

1 Bind the edges of your fabric with masking tape or oversew to prevent fraying. Fold the fabric into quarters to find the centre and begin stitching here from the centre of the chart overleaf.

2 Work over two threads of linen or one block of Aida, using two strands of cotton (floss) for cross stitch and one for French knots, backstitching and outlining. Work the orange stars in star stitch (see page 102) with one strand. Sew on the star button with light grey thread, if you are using it.

3 When all stitching is complete, press your work carefully and frame as a picture (see page 102 for advice). Alternatively, back your embroidery with Christmas fabric and hang it from a decorative wire hanger.

Santa tree decoration

Each motif from the main sampler can be used separately for cards and gifts and you can use up odds and ends of threads, fabric and ribbon to create lovely tree decorations. The decoration shown here is stitched over two threads of white 28-count linen with two blue star buttons added. See page 103 for making up the decoration. Look at the seasons section of the Motif Library for more Christmas motifs, particularly page 85.

Pick 'n' Mix

This sampler is perfect for substituting other festive and seasonal motifs from the Motif Library. For example, try working the two Christmas puddings from page 86 instead of the three stars and checked pattern in the bottom left corner. See page 6 for Will It Fit?

MERRY CHRISTMAS
PRESENTS JOY SANTA
FATHER CHRISTMAS
NOEL STOCKING TREES
TOYS
FOR YOU

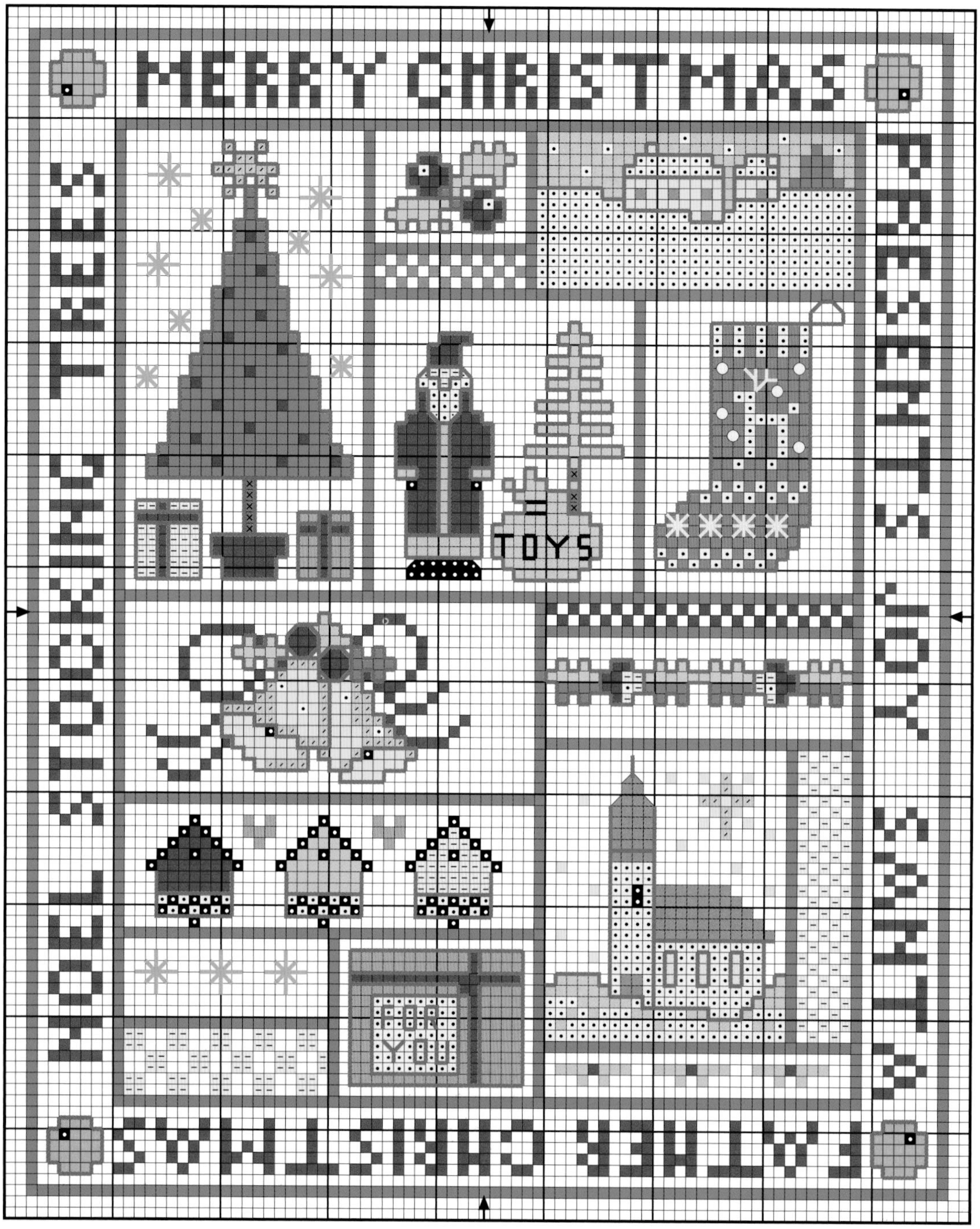

Very Merry Christmas

DMC stranded cotton

Cross stitch

• 310	414	/ 422	502	– 778	954	3822
340	415	× 435	740	793	3721	• ecru

Backstitch
- 310
- 414
- 740 (star stitch)
- ecru

French knots
- ○ ecru

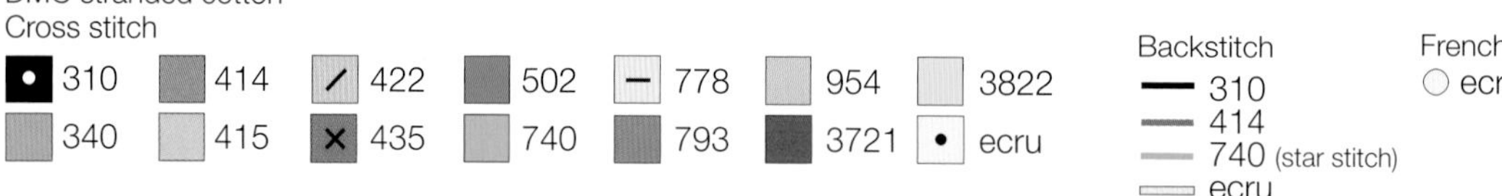

Slice of Life

The multi-boxes in Sampler Template 6 are very adaptable and ideal for creating very individual samplers about people's lives and passions and your family and friends will be delighted to receive such a thoughtful gift. Four sampler plans are shown here to give you ideas. See pages 5–7 for using and adapting the templates.

My Favourite Things...

This design shows how easy it is to make a very personal sampler for a friend. Simply choose a figure to represent the person and find motifs from the Motif Library relating to their hobbies and interests to fill in the boxes. The motifs here come from the home and work sections. You could also change the colour of the sampler template to your friend's favourite colour. Adding words in the border and beside the motifs really helps to make this sampler personal and expresses the varied interests and hobbies of the recipient. Adding the initials of their family members brings further interest. To add lettering, use the alphabets on page 90 and 91 and follow the instructions on page 5.

Bats 'n' Balls...

This design would make a wonderful gift for the sports-mad man in your life, perhaps for father's day or a birthday. There are many ways you can add personal interest to this sampler, for example you could stitch the scarf in their team colours or change the words around the outside to the name of their cricket or football club. See page 5 for instructions on how to chart and stitch lettering. You will find all the motifs in this sampler in the leisure section of the Motif Library.

Girl's World...

This girly sampler has all the elements to delight any little starlet. In delicious shades of pink and lavender on a white background it includes a teddy bear, presents, tiara, hearts and of course stars. The words capture some of the starlet's interests but you could make these more personal. All the motifs can be found in the leisure and home sections of the Motif Library. The black dots on the hearts show where sparkling beads could bring extra texture to the design. You could add a little girl's name and birthday to this design (see page 5 for stitching lettering and numbers).

Bon Voyage...

This design in bold colour combinations is the perfect gift for someone who enjoys travelling. The motifs are from the leisure and work sections of the Motif Library. The plane shows how a motif can break into the template to create additional visual impact. Don't be afraid to change the shape of some motifs to better fit the design. A Bon Voyage message and simple border motifs fill the remaining areas. You can choose other motifs, for example, put in different flags, alter the words (see page 5 for working lettering), or add a greeting, place name or date to the sampler.

Happy Families

This sampler celebrates the family with a big bright design using Sampler Template 7 (page 98). I wanted to stitch a sampler that included lots of family details, with pictures of the family at the top, and their home and pets, names, wedding and birth dates. To personalize this sampler use the Motif Library and alter the people, motifs and wording to those appropriate to your family. See page 7 for two smaller versions of this sampler, to give you ideas on how easy it is to adapt the template. A Christmas sampler on page 31 has been stitched using the same plan.

Stitch count 185 x 101 Design size 33.5 x 18.3cm (13¼ x 7½in)

You will need

- 49 x 33cm (19 x 13in) 28-count linen or 14-count Aida in white
- DMC stranded cotton (floss) as in the chart key
- Size 26 tapestry needle

1 First work out the name and dates you wish to include on squared paper using a pencil and eraser, using the alphabets and numbers charted on page 90.

2 Bind the edges of your fabric with masking tape or oversew to prevent fraying. Fold the fabric into quarters to find the centre and begin stitching here from the centre of the chart overleaf. The chart is split into two parts. If you wish, you could photocopy both parts and tape them together.

3 Work over two threads of linen or one block of Aida, using two strands of cotton (floss) for cross stitch and one for backstitching and French knots.

4 If you want to make the sampler more personal, choose other motifs from the Motif Library. Stitch your family details in the boxes you have chosen (see Adding Words, page 5).

5 When all stitching is complete, press your work carefully and frame as a picture (see page 102 for advice).

Welcome card

This charming card is quick to stitch over one block of white 14-count Aida and it's easy to choose a different house from the Motif Library or add a row of hearts or flowers above and below the design. Use the alphabets on pages 90 and 91 to customize your design.

Pick 'n' Mix

If the family you are stitching the sampler for have pets other than a dog then choose another motif from the library – perhaps a cat or goldfish or chart your own pet. See page 6 for Will It Fit? and page 7 for Charting Your Own Motifs.

our
FAMILY
IS A CIRCLE OF LOVE
ABCDEFGHIJKL
MNOPQRSTUV
WXYZ123
POLLY JOHNSON JAMES BLAKE
WERE MARRIED 10 SEPTEMBER 1994
1995
JOSH
1997
HARRIET
2000
SAM
2003
ELLIE
PLUM TREE COTTAGE
Bless Our Family

TOP

Happy Families
DMC stranded cotton
Cross stitch

413, 414, 472, 598, 725, 754, 809, 825, 913, 3607, 3608, 3747, ecru, 51 variegated, 107 variegated, 125 variegated

Backstitch
414, 645, 809, 825, ecru, 107 variegated, 125 variegated

French knots
414, 645, ecru

BOTTOM

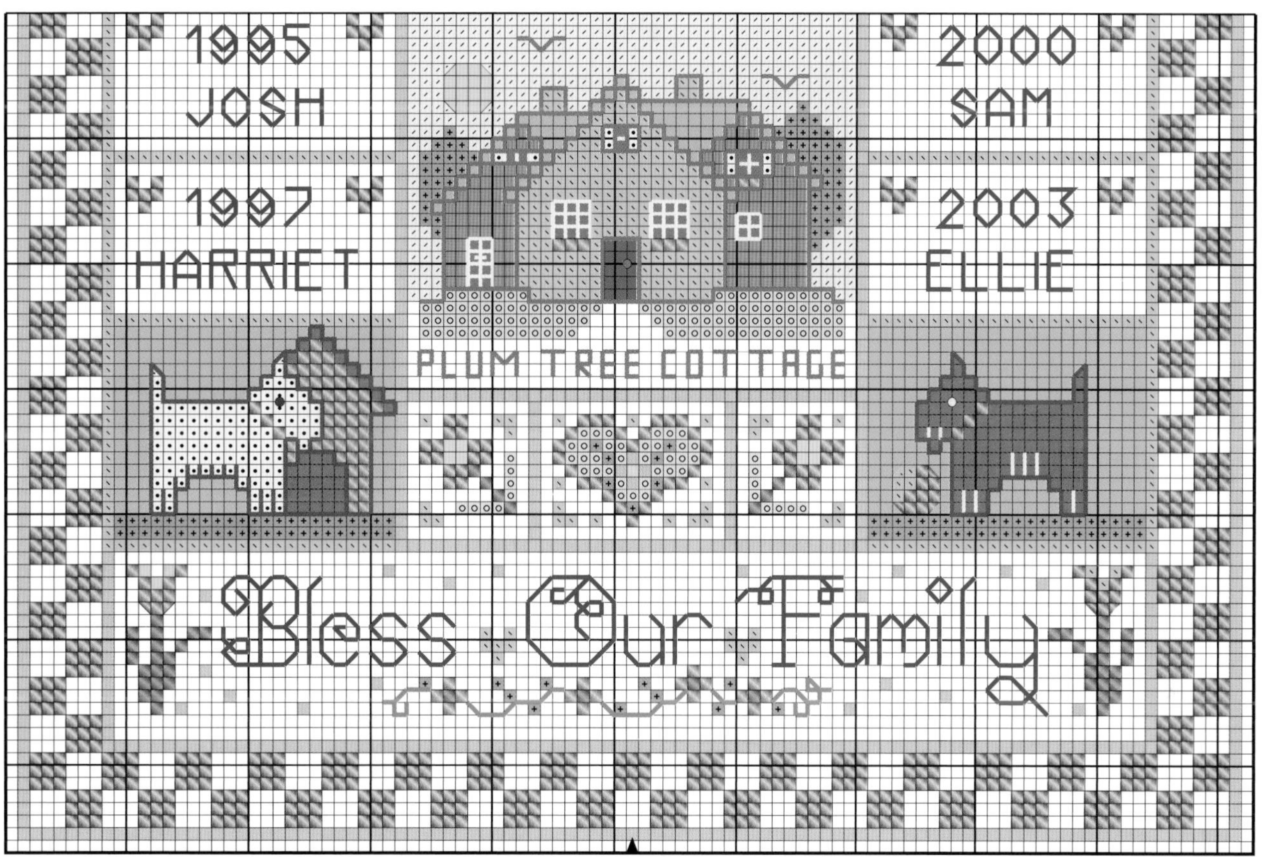

This Christmas sampler and its plan show how versatile Template 7 is. It is filled with lots of charming festive motifs – all from the seasons section of the Motif Library, page 78–88.

Holiday Memories

The idea of making a memory sampler appealed to me, as people often keep souvenirs of loved ones and special occasions, and this is a way to use stitching to display them. This holiday memories sampler uses Sampler Template 8 (page 100), which I've designed to be very adaptable for maximum creativity. It allows you to include quite large motifs, such as the seaside hotel scene shown here, plus some long, deep bands which can be filled with repeated motifs like palm trees or sailing boats or a collection of small items like shells. The details of the holiday are recorded using the alphabet on page 90. Stitched examples of other memories samplers are shown on pages 35–37.

Stitch count 121 x 72 Design size 22 x 13cm (8½ x 5¼in)

You will need

- 38 x 30cm (15 x 12in) 28-count linen or 14-count Aida in white
- DMC stranded cotton (floss) as in the chart key
- Size 26 tapestry needle
- Tiny shells (optional)

1 Using the alphabet chart on page 90, work out your name and holiday details on squared paper with pencil and eraser (see page 5).

2 Bind the edges of your fabric with masking tape or oversew to prevent fraying. Fold the fabric into quarters to find the centre and begin stitching here from the centre of the chart overleaf.

3 Work over two threads of linen or one block of Aida, using two strands of cotton (floss) for cross stitch and one for backstitching and outlining.

4 When all the stitching is complete, press your work and then glue on the tiny shells or other holiday mementoes with fabric glue. Finally, frame your work as a picture, without glass if you've used three-dimensional objects (see page 102 for framing advice).

Photo album

Two simple motifs and some lettering from the main sampler stitched on white 14-count stitching paper make a perfect patch to display on a photograph album. Trim the finished embroidery and glue it to the front of a clear plastic photo album.

Pick 'n' Mix

There are many motifs in the Motif Library that could be used to change the Holiday Memories sampler, particularly in the leisure section. For example, you could use the ballooning picture from page 61 or the 'life's a beach' motif from page 66 instead of the hotel scene and shells. See page 6 for Will It Fit? and Creating Mirror Images.

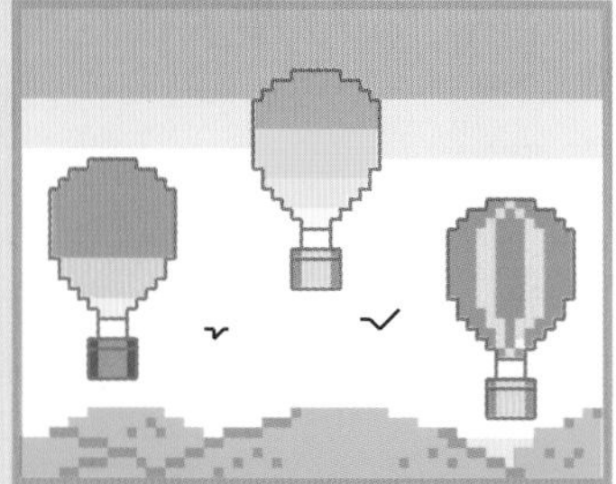

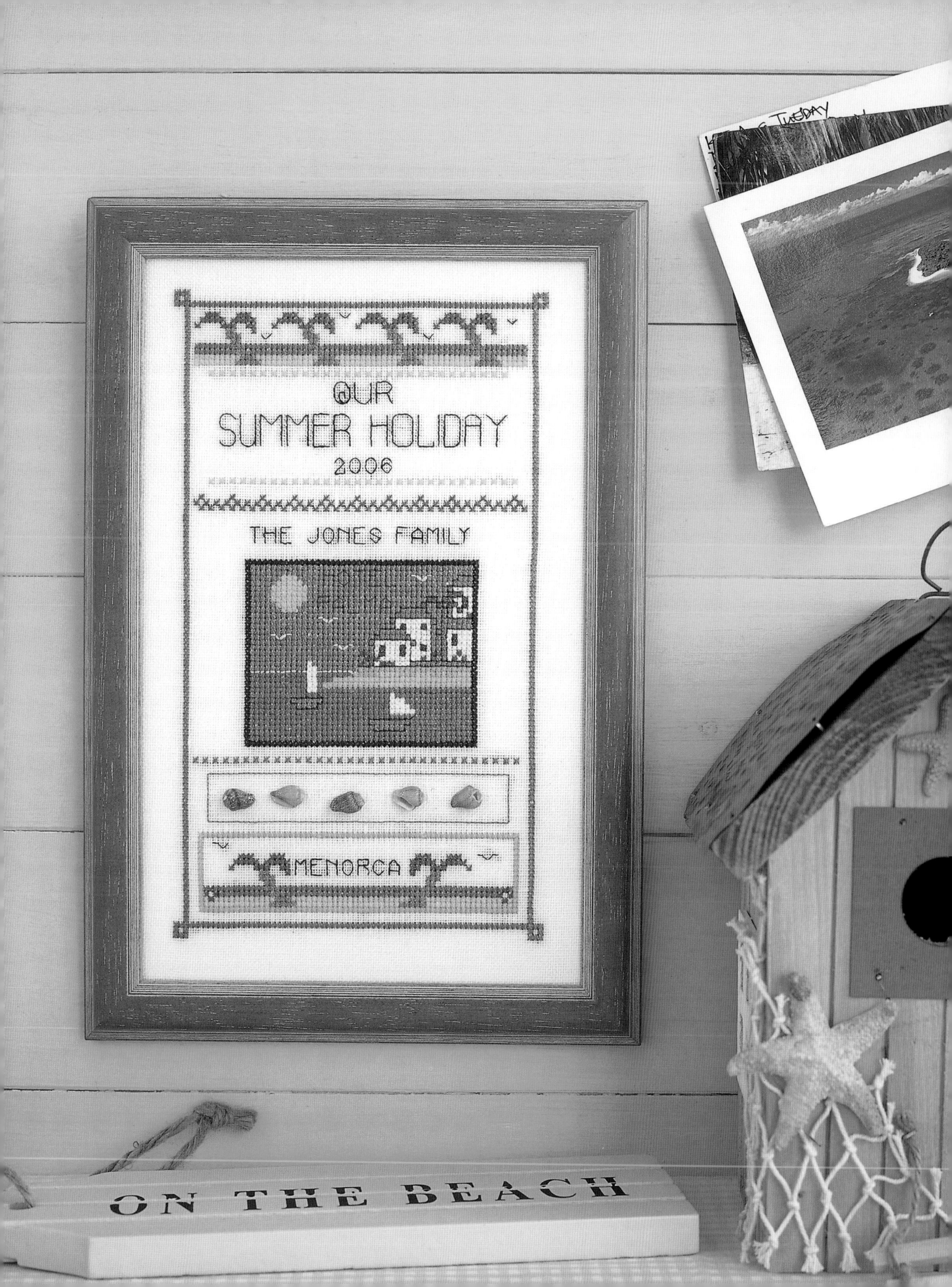
OUR
SUMMER HOLIDAY
2006
THE JONES FAMILY
MENORCA
ON THE BEACH

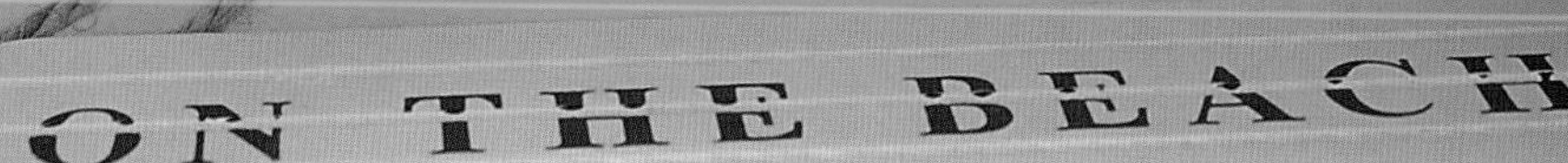

Holiday Memories
DMC stranded cotton
Cross stitch

- 318
- 414
- 436
- 444
- 702
- 809
- 824
- 972
- 996
- 3804
- • blanc

Backstitch

- 414
- 444
- 702
- 809
- 824
- 3804
- blanc

Pick 'n' Mix

You could stitch different motifs in this template, perhaps to bring back memories of a holiday nearer home – what about using the row of beach huts from page 60 or the waves and starfish borders from page 81? You could also feature a favourite holiday photo in the centre of the sampler, as I've done on page 37 with a picture of a much-loved relative.

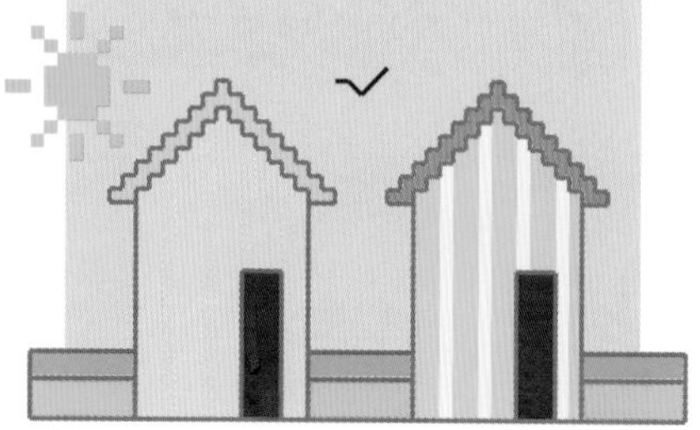

Down Memory Lane

Using Sampler Template 8 (page 100) as a starting point, you can get really creative and produce a memory sampler of your own. Try adding small objects like badges, charms, rings or photographs to preserve and display them in an unusual way. Choose suitable motifs from the Motif Library to illustrate your sampler and use the alphabets on pages 90 and 91 to work out the wording. Depending on the amount of information or decoration you wish to include, you can vary the length of this sampler to fit your requirements.

Romantic Memories

This design was specially created to celebrate the romantic meeting in Italy of a couple who later married. A small, stylized picture of the Duomo in Florence was used as the focal point for the design. You could create your own picture of a special view (see page 7 for charting your own motifs). To add to the Italian atmosphere, grapes and grapevines make a decorative border and at the bottom of the design is a big yellow sunflower. Why not replace some of the cross stitch with gleaming beads, such as on the grapes here? To keep the romantic theme a heart charm is included. You could create your own sampler celebrating a romantic meeting by changing the names, place and dates, and adding a picture or motif to represent the place. The motifs used in this sampler can be found in the home and garden and leisure sections of the Motif Library.

Military Memories

This sampler was created to preserve a special military badge, and to record the name of the person it belongs to and the date they joined the merchant navy. It could easily be used with any kind of badge or logo – perhaps to mark a retirement or long service celebration. The motifs used are from the leisure section of the Motif Library but you could work different motifs to symbolize the person's employment. Plan the name and dates using the alphabets on pages 90 and 91. The anchor charms add a nice touch but you could also preserve wartime memorabilia, like cap badges, RAF wings and other uniform badges that many families have stored away. Why not make them into a picture and create a truly memorable family heirloom?

Vintage Memories

This pretty design has an antique look about it because it was designed to display an old photo of a much-loved relative. The photograph becomes a very special keepsake by adding it to a sampler with the relative's name and date of birth and delicate pansies for a traditional decorative appearance (from the home section of the Motif Library). You could stitch this design to incorporate your own antique photo, just by changing the name and date (see page 5 for instructions on how to create the lettering).

Motif Library

The following pages have a huge selection of motifs covering a wide range of subjects for you to substitute for motifs in the stitch-off-the-page samplers or to create your own samplers from scratch. Let the sampler plans provided throughout the book inspire you to make unique samplers of your own. Alternatively, stitch the motifs separately for quick cards and gifts, like those shown opposite and in the sampler chapters. All the motifs are suitable for 14-count Aida or 28-count evenweave fabric. The colours charted in the library can be changed to shades of your own choosing.

The Chart Keys

Whether the motifs you use are stitched directly from the Motif Library, or are already charted within a stitch-off-the-page sampler, always refer to the chart key provided for that specific library page or sampler – see Using Chart Keys, page 4.

JULY 4th
Welcome to our Patch
I
MY
DOG

Family
NO.1
MUM
NO.1
DAD
Families are tied
together
with heart-strings

DMC stranded cotton
Cross stitch
209
310
317
351
415
436
518
613
740
793
809
825
913
3608
3779
3820
3823
3846
ecru
Backstitch
317
351
793
825
913
3608
ecru
French knots
317
351
825
THE
ROBINSONS

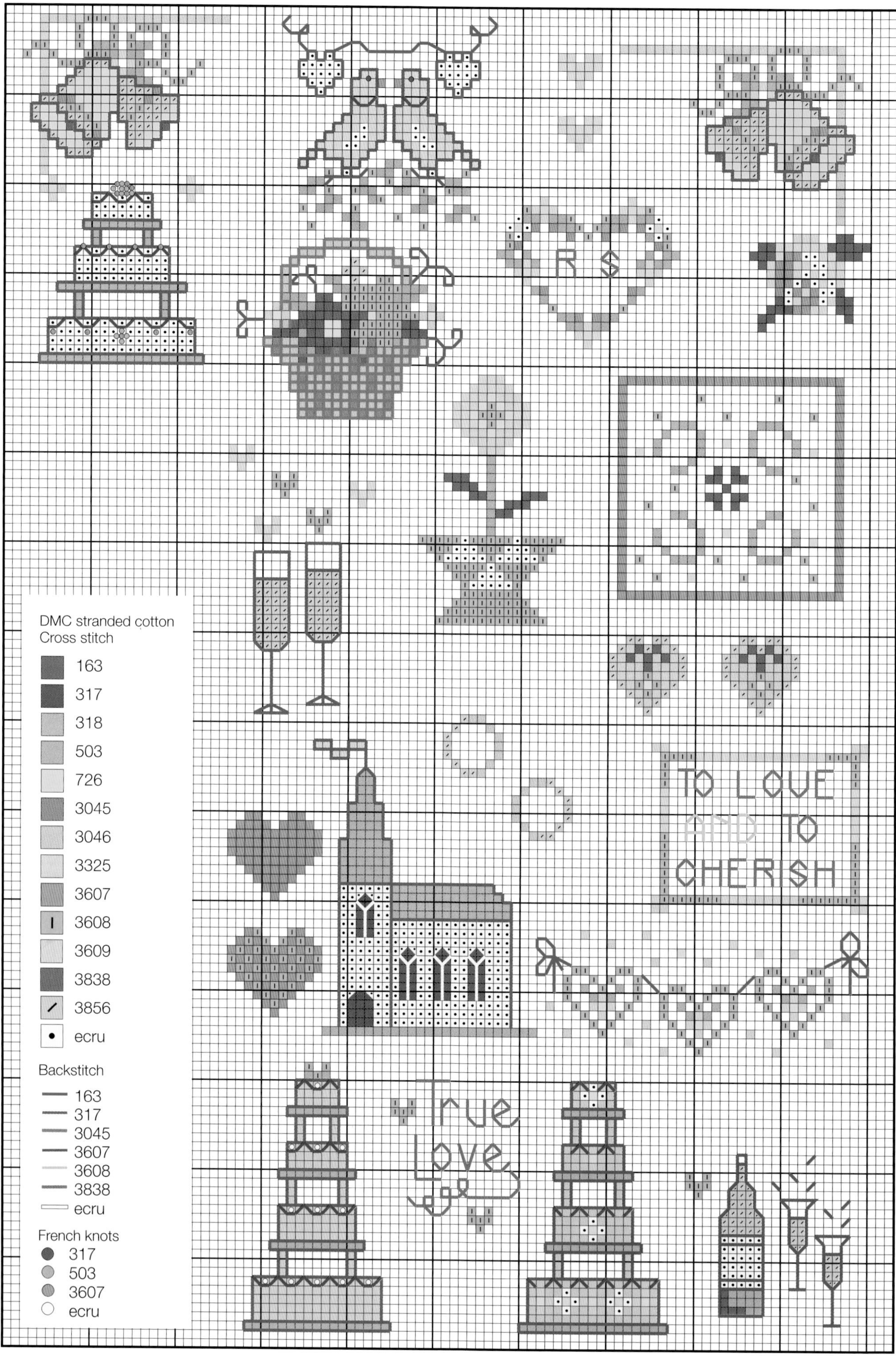
DMC stranded cotton
Cross stitch
163
317
318
503
726
3045
3046
3325
3607
3608
3609
3838
3856
ecru
Backstitch
163
317
3045
3607
3608
3838
ecru
French knots
317
503
3607
ecru
R S
TO LOVE
AND TO
CHERISH
True
Love

DMC stranded cotton
Cross stitch
210
317
340
341
352
437
553
605
744
754
3607
3608
3766
3839
ecru
Backstitch
317
351
352
553
907
3608
3839
French knots
317
553
ecru
TOYS
A
B
C
SAM
2-1-06
ROCK-A-BYE
ELLIE
1-6-06
Bless the
BABY

JUNE 6 2006
WEDDING
CONGRATULATIONS
SOPHIE AND DANIEL
WEDDING
Congratulations
Blessings on your
CHRISTENING
WITH LOVE
ON YOUR
WEDDING
DAY
DMC stranded cotton
Cross stitch
163
318
351
352
353
597
726
799
964
3325
3607
3608
3609
3838
3839
3856
ecru
Backstitch
317
3607
3838
ecru
French knots
317
ecru

Grandparents are SPECIAL!
TWINS are twice as NICE!
WE GRANDMA'S COOKIES TEA
BEST AUNT
AUNTIE LINDA
BEST UNCLE
UNCLE BOB
DMC stranded cotton
Cross stitch
209
317
351
353
415
436
613
732
743
794
825
954
3608
3820
ecru
Backstitch
317
French knots
317
351
ecru

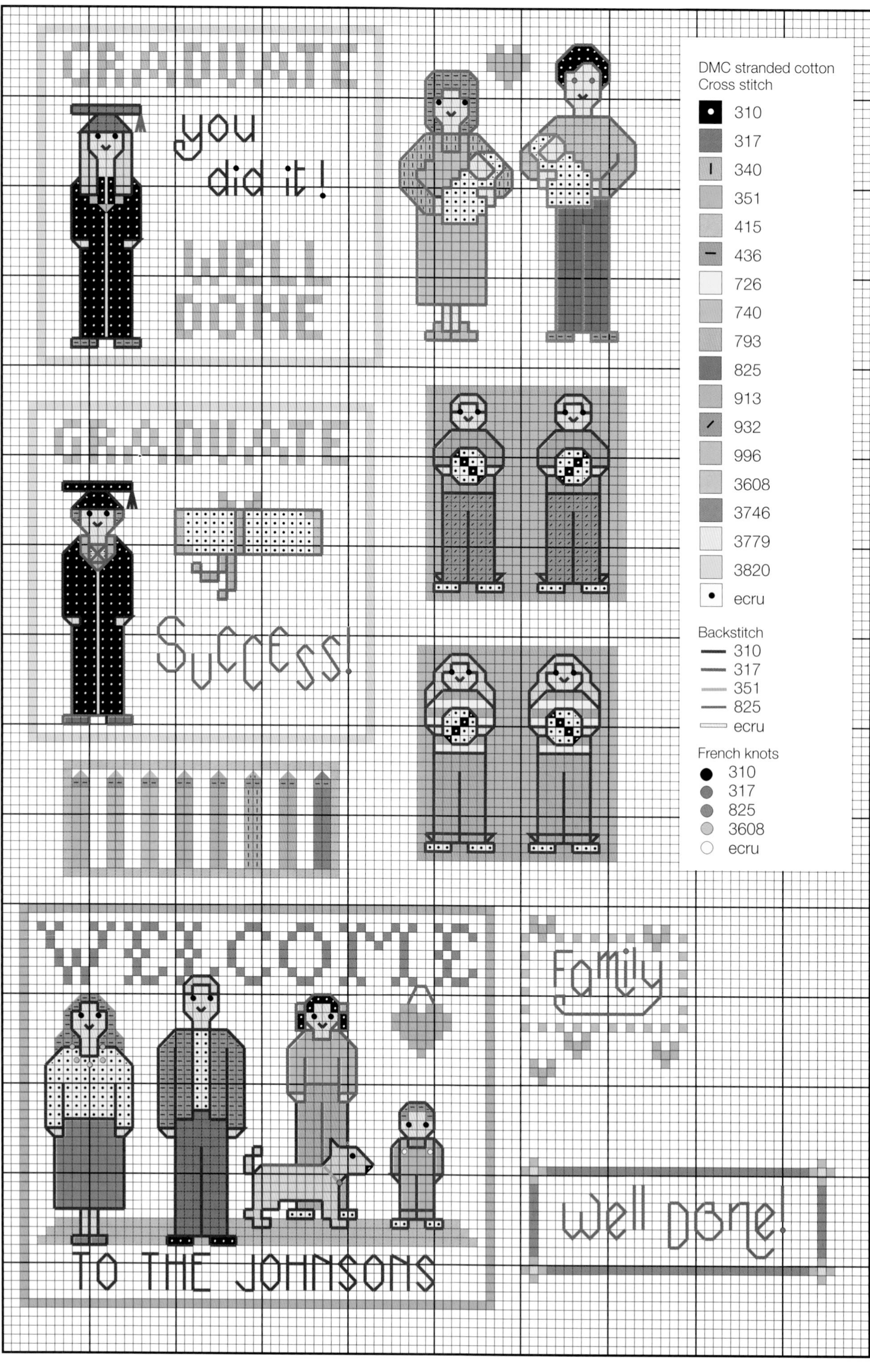

GRADUATE
you did it!
WELL DONE
GRADUATE
Success!
WELCOME
TO THE JOHNSONS
Family
Well Done!
DMC stranded cotton
Cross stitch
310
317
340
351
415
436
726
740
793
825
913
932
996
3608
3746
3779
3820
ecru
Backstitch
310
317
351
825
ecru
French knots
310
317
825
3608
ecru

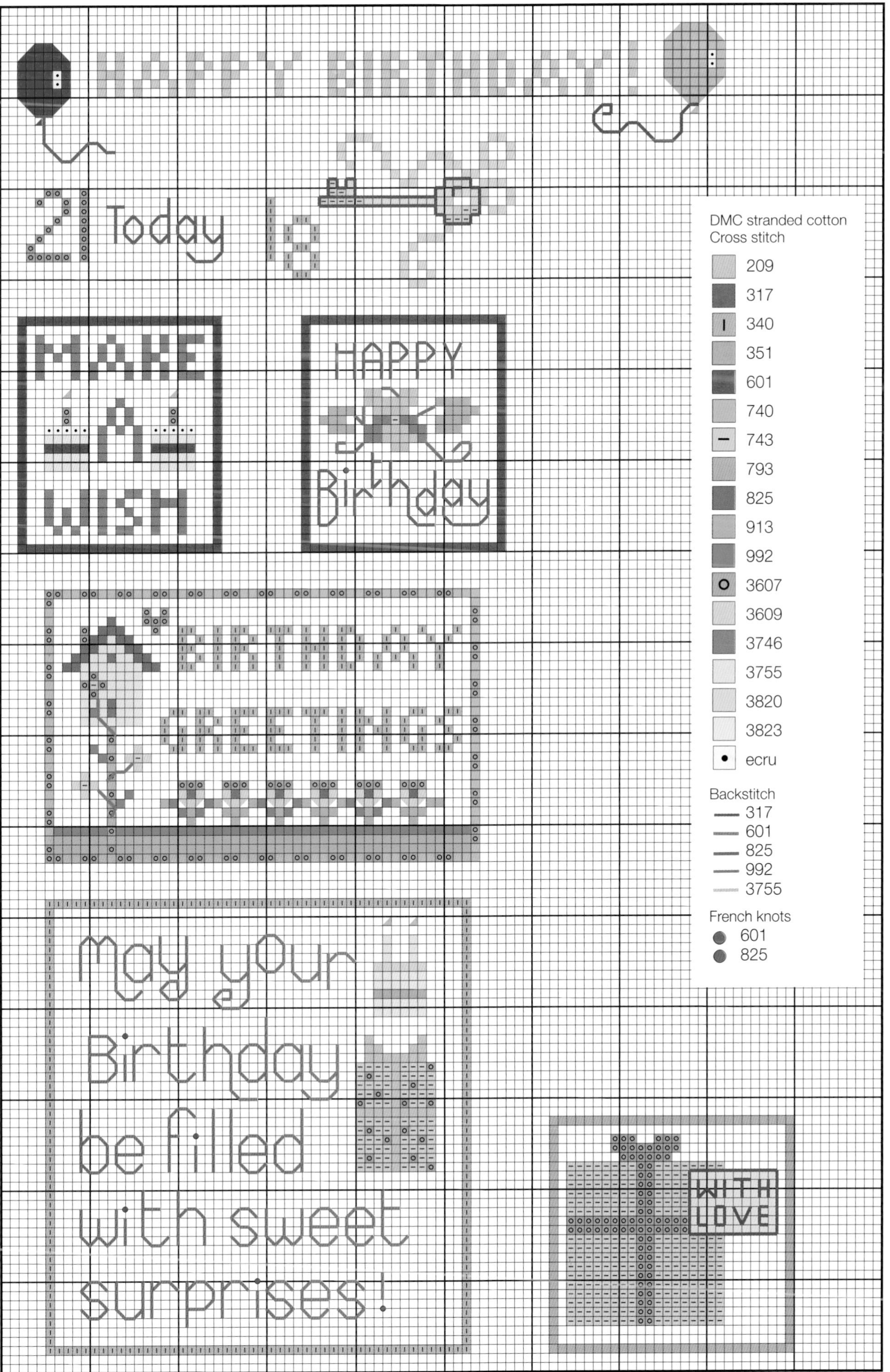
HAPPY BIRTHDAY!
Today
MAKE A WISH
HAPPY Birthday
BIRTHDAY GREETINGS
May your Birthday be filled with sweet surprises!
WITH LOVE
DMC stranded cotton
Cross stitch
209
317
340
351
601
740
743
793
825
913
992
3607
3609
3746
3755
3820
3823
ecru
Backstitch
317
601
825
992
3755
French knots
601
825

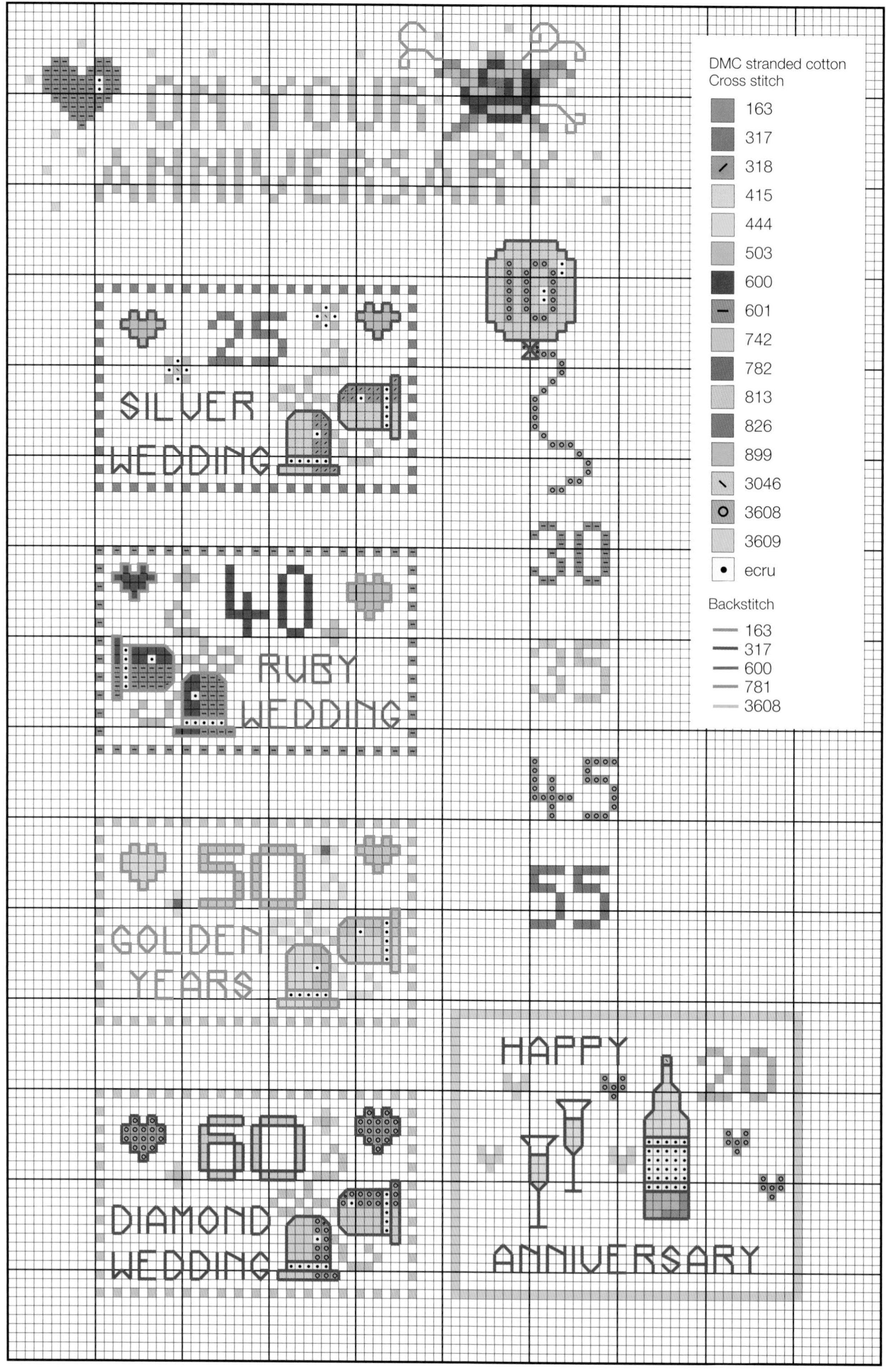
ON YOUR ANNIVERSARY
25
SILVER WEDDING
40
RUBY WEDDING
50
GOLDEN YEARS
60
DIAMOND WEDDING
30
35
45
55
HAPPY 20 ANNIVERSARY
DMC stranded cotton
Cross stitch
163
317
318
415
444
503
600
601
742
782
813
826
899
3046
3608
3609
ecru
Backstitch
163
317
600
781
3608

A new Baby is
A FAMILY
Treasure
CONGRATULATIONS
ON YOUR
ENGAGEMENT
STITCHED
WITH
LOVE
Birthday
Blessings
Bless our
GRANDCHILDREN
CATHERINE
ANDREW
WITH
LOVE
STITCHED
BY:
DMC stranded cotton
Cross stitch
125 variegated
209
317
340
350
351
353
552
704
794
798
3608
3823
3839
3856
ecru
Backstitch
125 variegated
317
798
3608
French knots
317

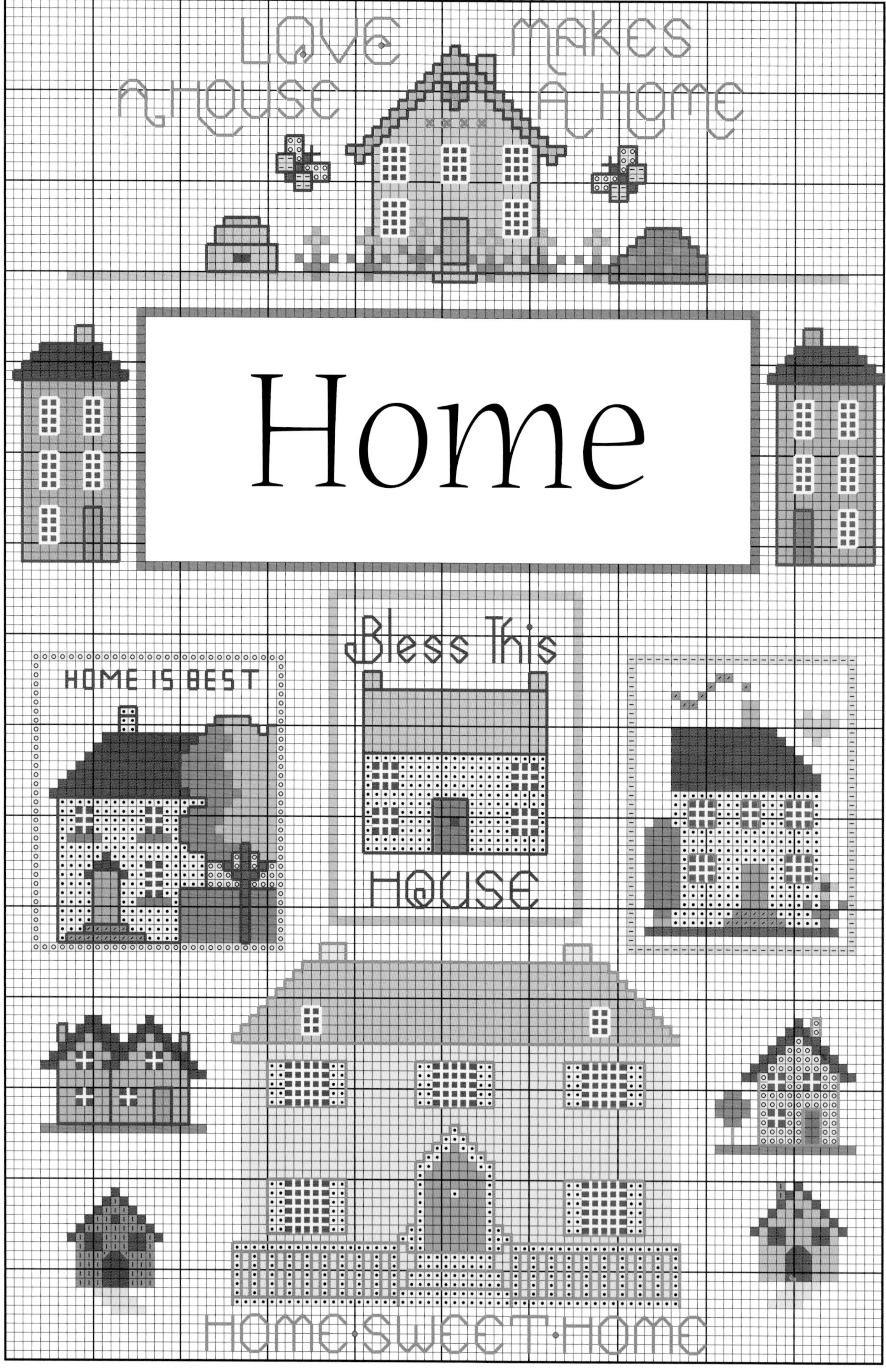
LOVE MAKES
A HOUSE A HOME
Home
Bless This
HOUSE
HOME IS BEST
HOME·SWEET·HOME

DMC stranded cotton
Cross stitch
209
317
318
351
415
437
553
666
741
799
813
841
894
905
907
3064
3689
3746
3823
ecru
Backstitch
317
318
351
741
907
3746
ecru
French knots
317
351
3746
ecru
HONEY
KITCHEN
SWEET
KITCHEN

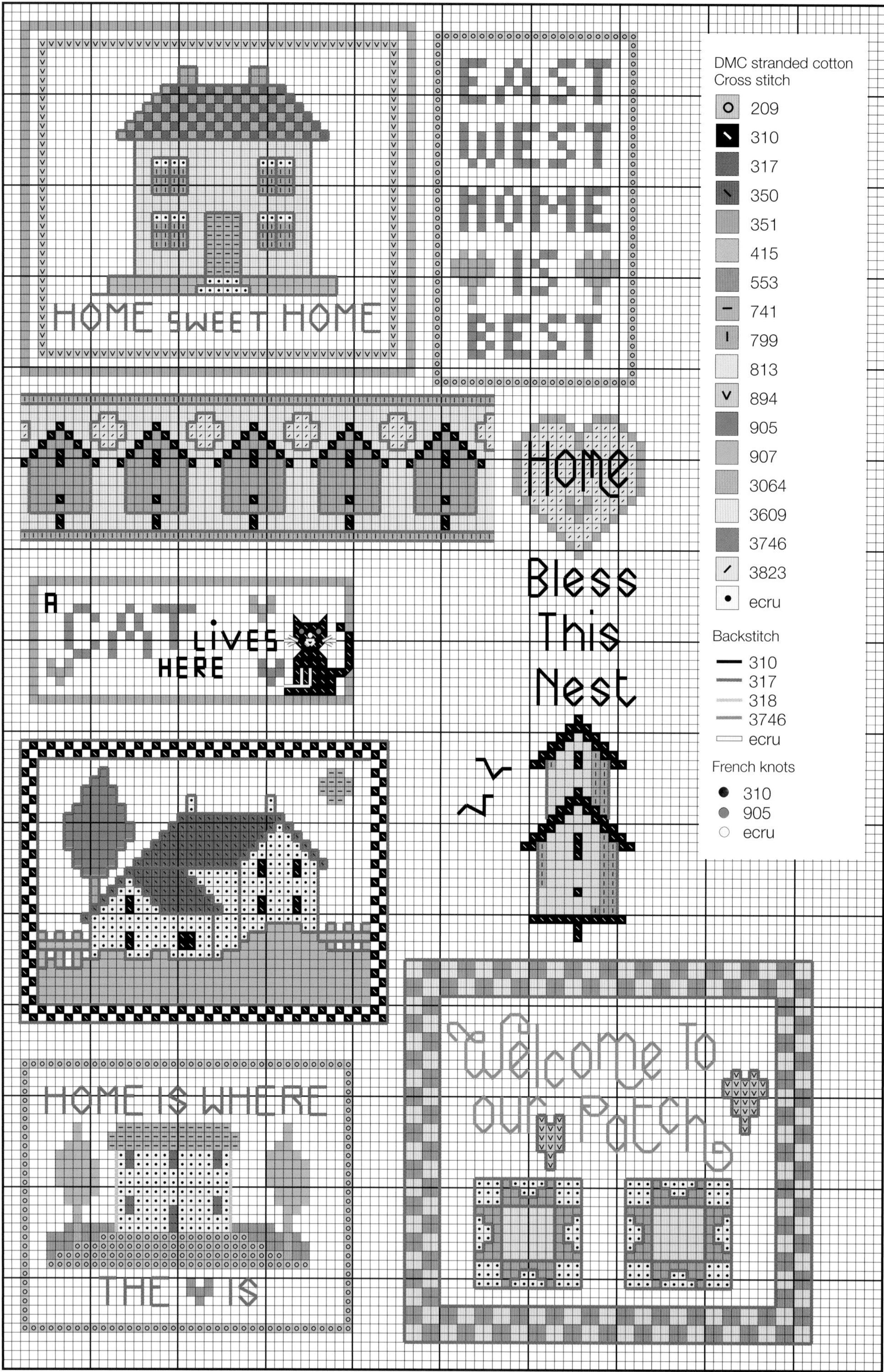
HOME sweet HOME
EAST
WEST
HOME
IS
BEST
Home
Bless
This
Nest
A CAT lives HERE
HOME IS WHERE
THE IS
Welcome To our Patch
DMC stranded cotton
Cross stitch
209
310
317
350
351
415
553
741
799
813
894
905
907
3064
3609
3746
3823
ecru
Backstitch
310
317
318
3746
ecru
French knots
310
905
ecru

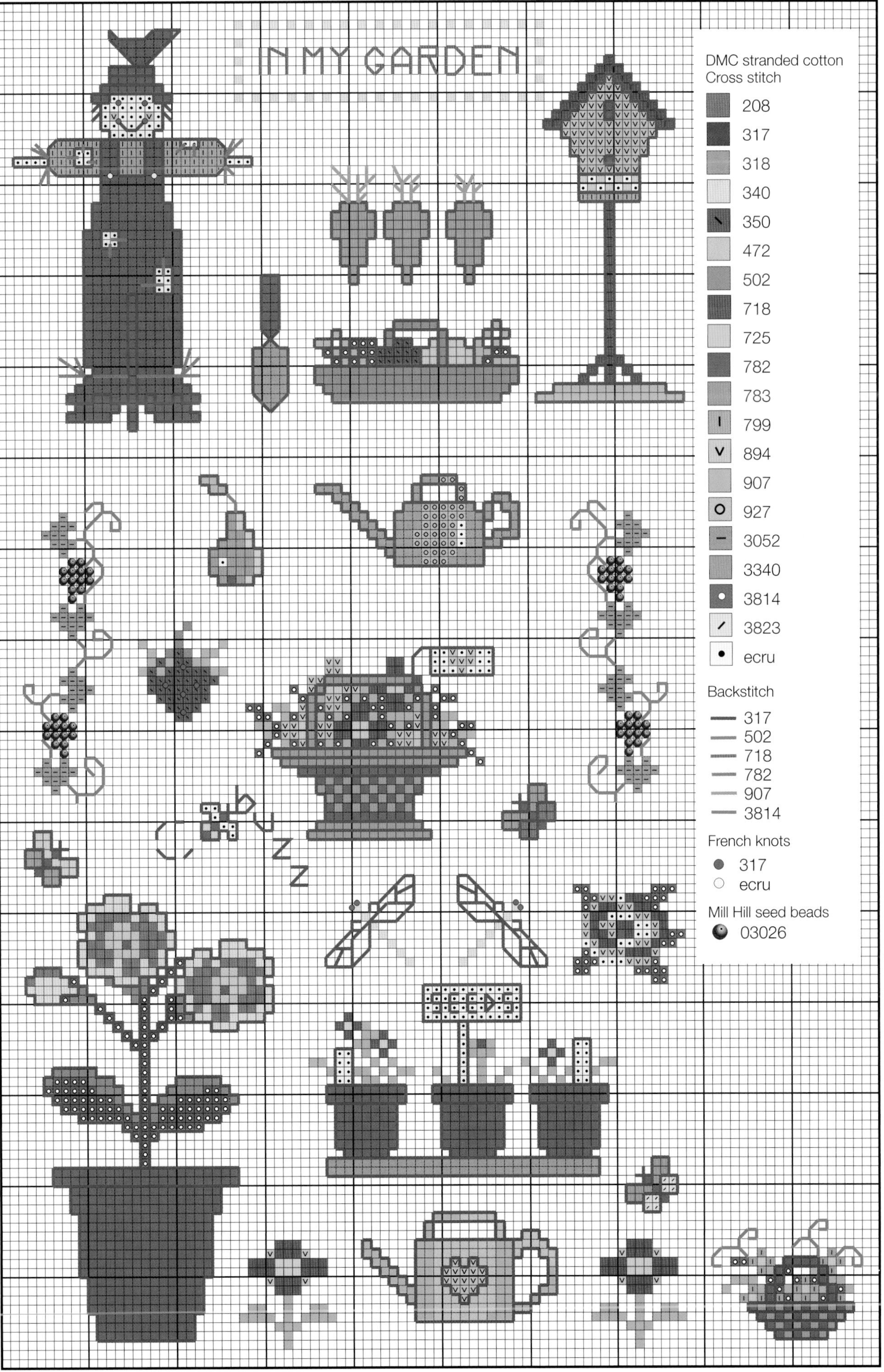
IN MY GARDEN
BUZZ
DMC stranded cotton
Cross stitch
208
317
318
340
350
472
502
718
725
782
783
799
894
907
927
3052
3340
3814
3823
ecru
Backstitch
317
502
718
782
907
3814
French knots
317
ecru
Mill Hill seed beads
03026

When friends meet
Hearts warm
PASTA LASAGNE
THANKS TO THE
COOK
WELCOME
TO OUR
HOME
HOME
is WHERE
THE is
DMC stranded cotton
Cross stitch
209
317
318
350
351
413
415
553
741
742
743
799
813
894
905
907
943
958
3047
3064
3325
ecru
Backstitch
317
413
ecru
French knots
413

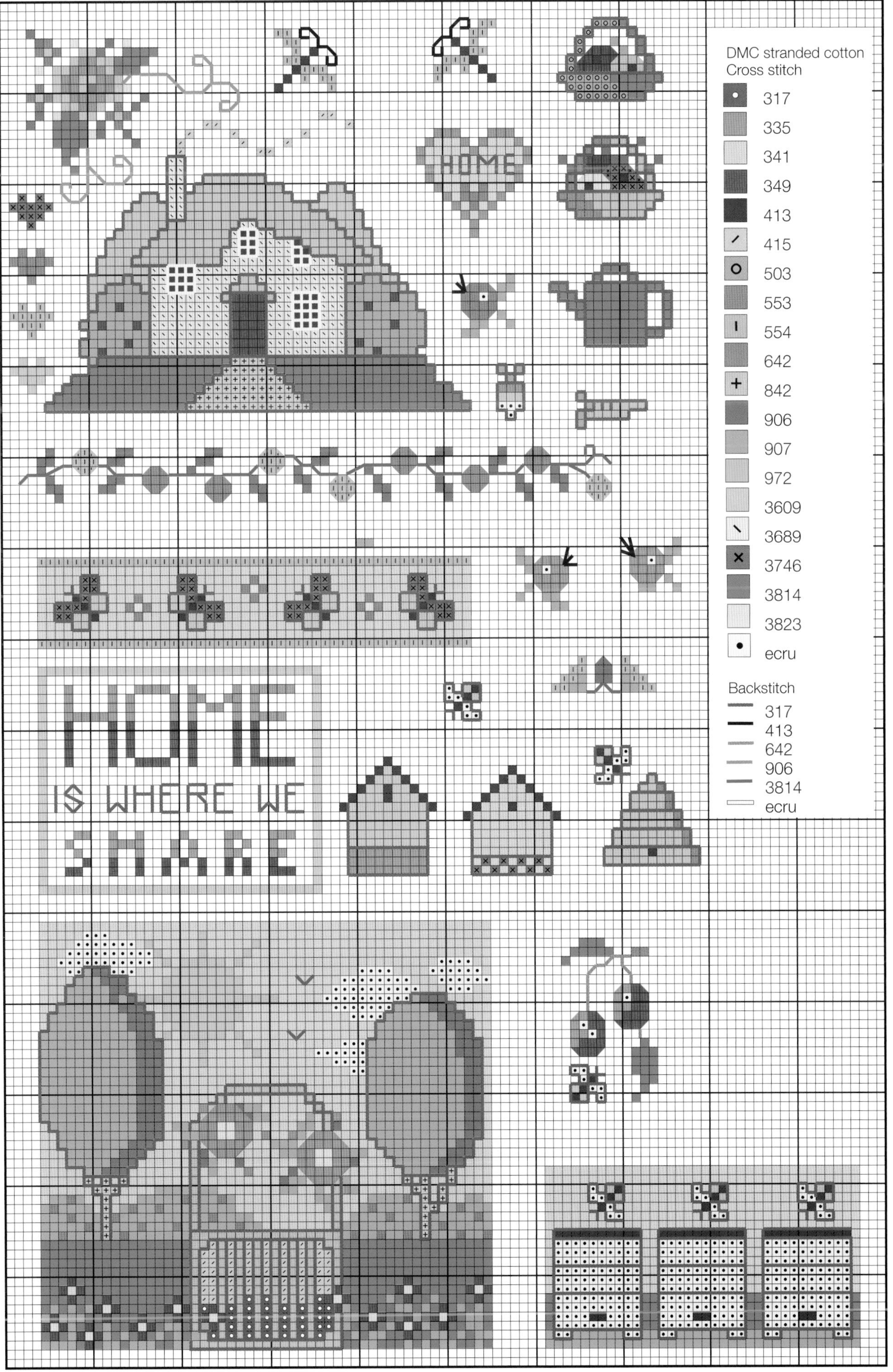
HOME
HOME
IS WHERE WE
SHARE
DMC stranded cotton
Cross stitch
317
335
341
349
413
415
503
553
554
642
842
906
907
972
3609
3689
3746
3814
3823
ecru
Backstitch
317
413
642
906
3814
ecru

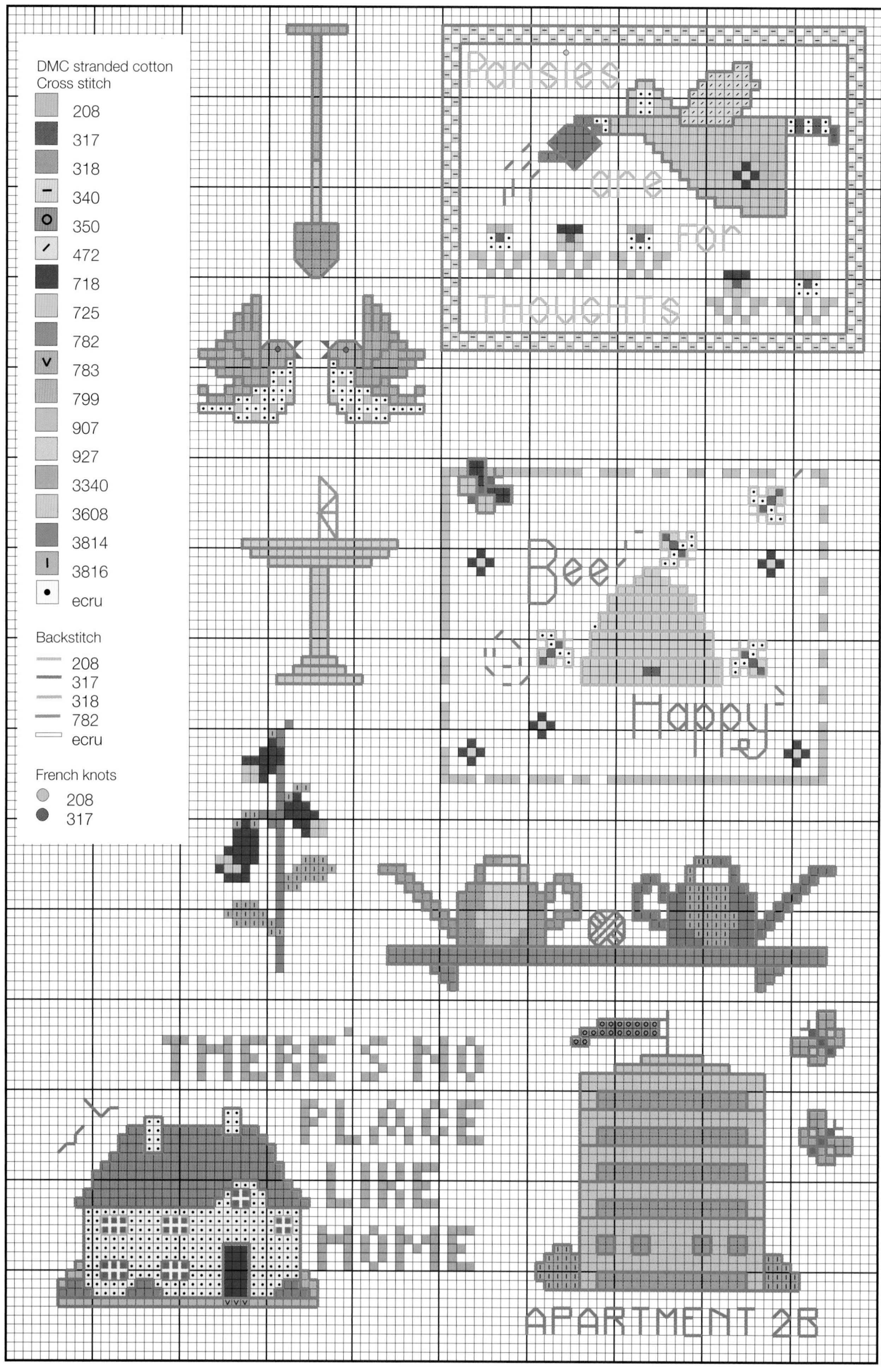
DMC stranded cotton
Cross stitch
208
317
318
340
350
472
718
725
782
783
799
907
927
3340
3608
3814
3816
ecru
Backstitch
208
317
318
782
ecru
French knots
208
317
Pansies are for thoughts
Bee Happy
THERE'S NO PLACE LIKE HOME
APARTMENT 2B

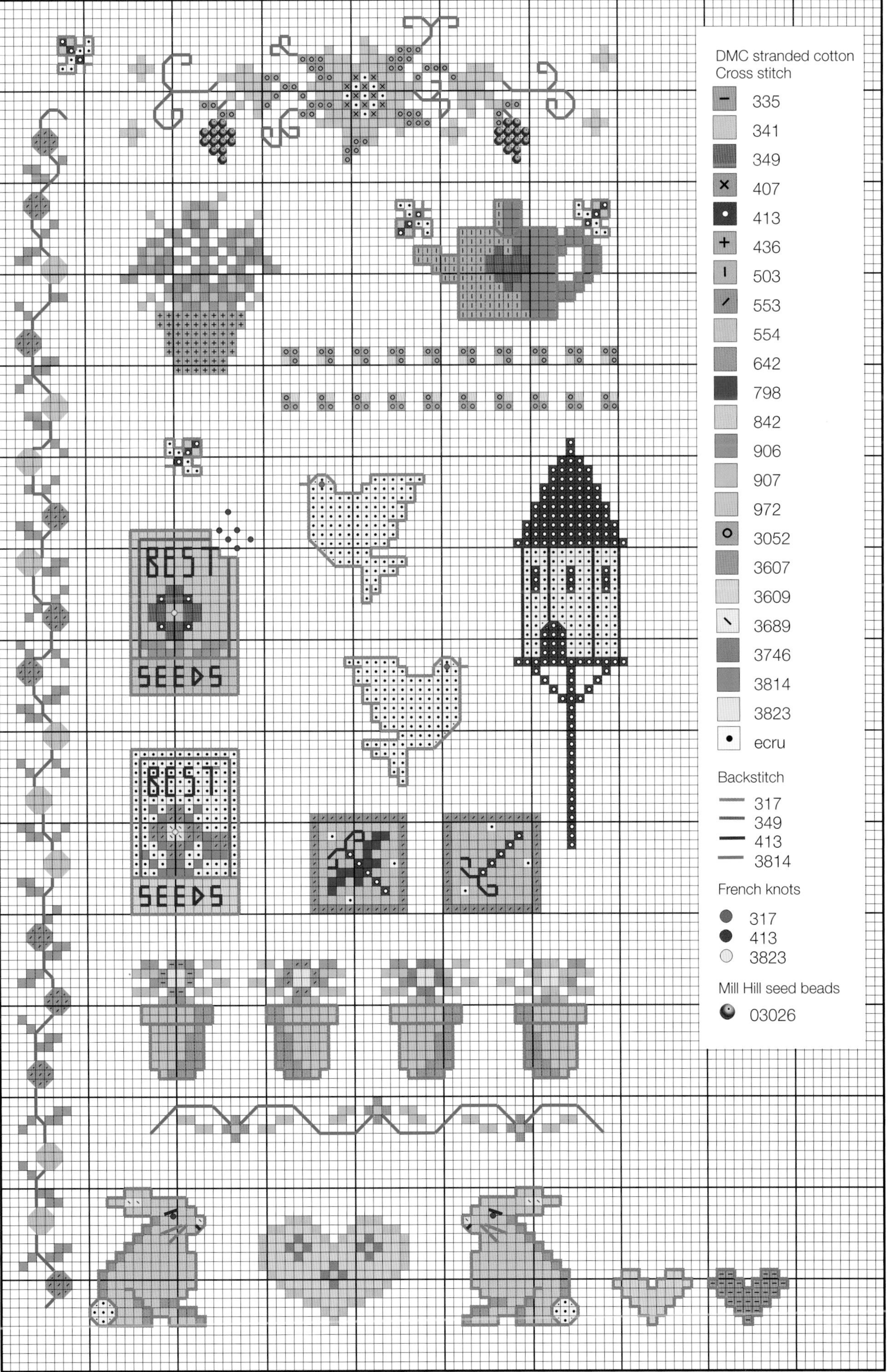
DMC stranded cotton
Cross stitch
335
341
349
407
413
436
503
553
554
642
798
842
906
907
972
3052
3607
3609
3689
3746
3814
3823
ecru
Backstitch
317
349
413
3814
French knots
317
413
3823
Mill Hill seed beads
03026
BEST
SEEDS
BEST
SEEDS

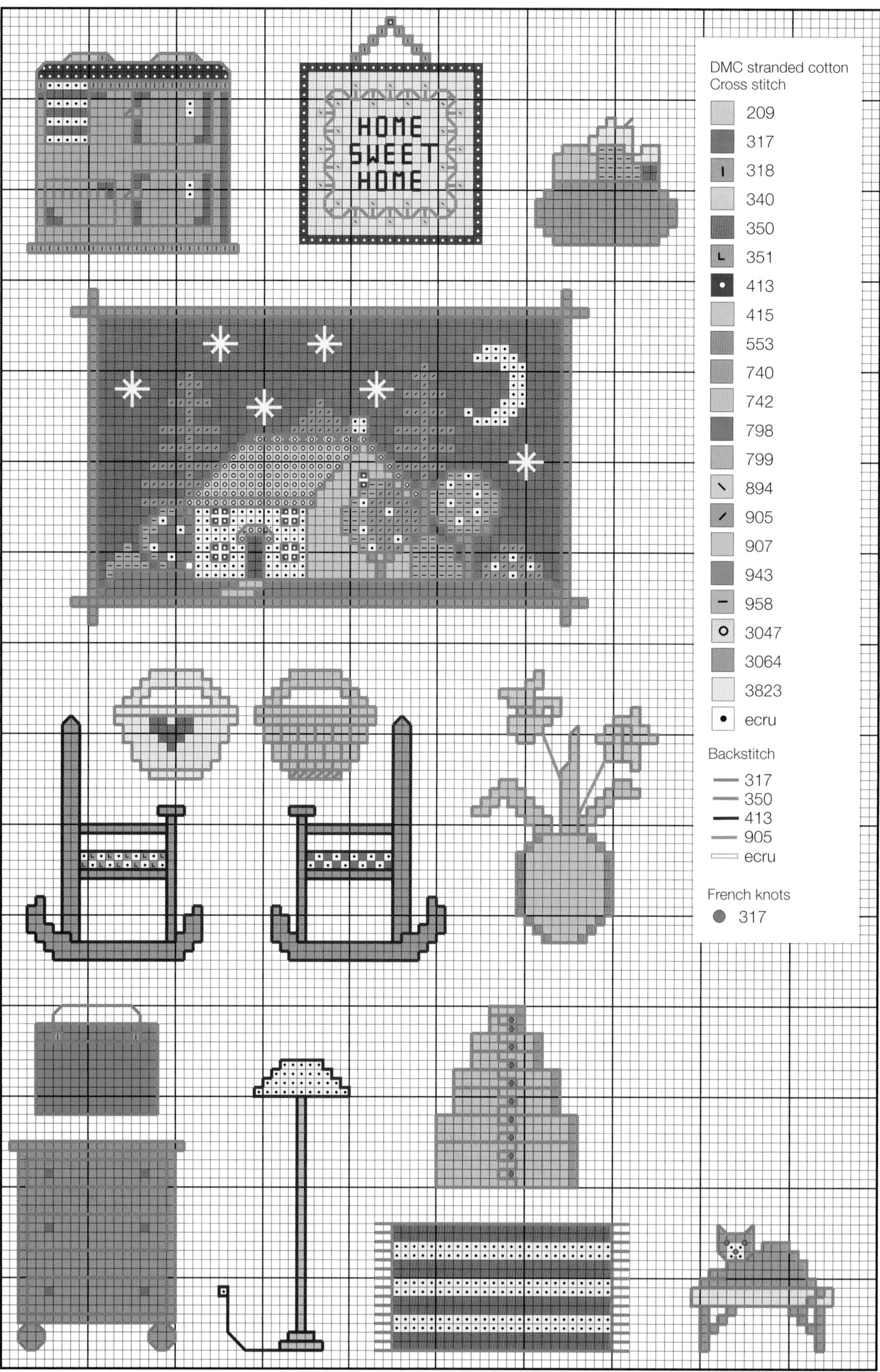
HOME
SWEET
HOME
DMC stranded cotton
Cross stitch
209
317
318
340
350
351
413
415
553
740
742
798
799
894
905
907
943
958
3047
3064
3823
ecru
Backstitch
317
350
413
905
ecru
French knots
317

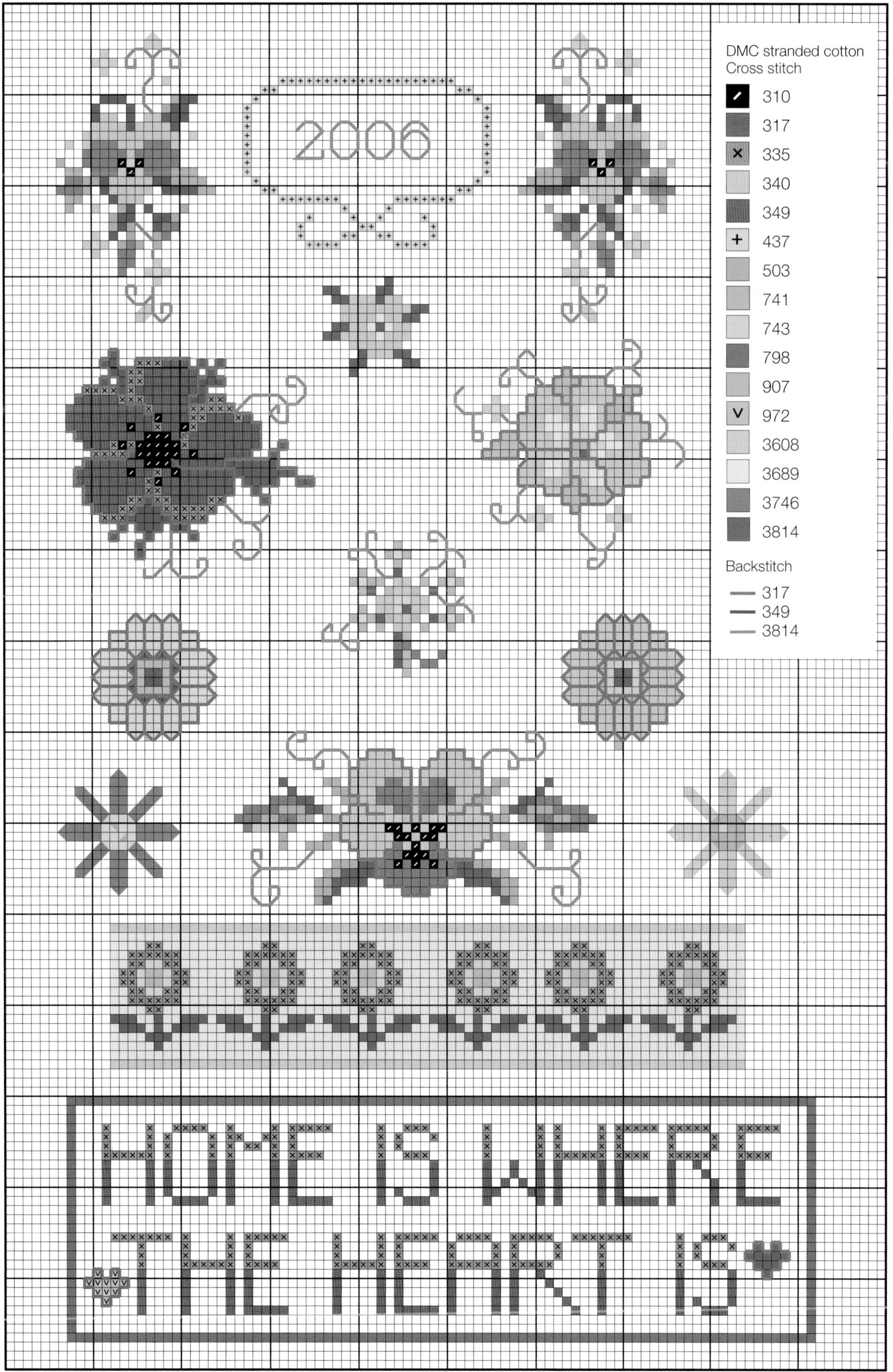
2006
HOME IS WHERE
THE HEART IS
DMC stranded cotton
Cross stitch
310
317
335
340
349
437
503
741
743
798
907
972
3608
3689
3746
3814
Backstitch
317
349
3814

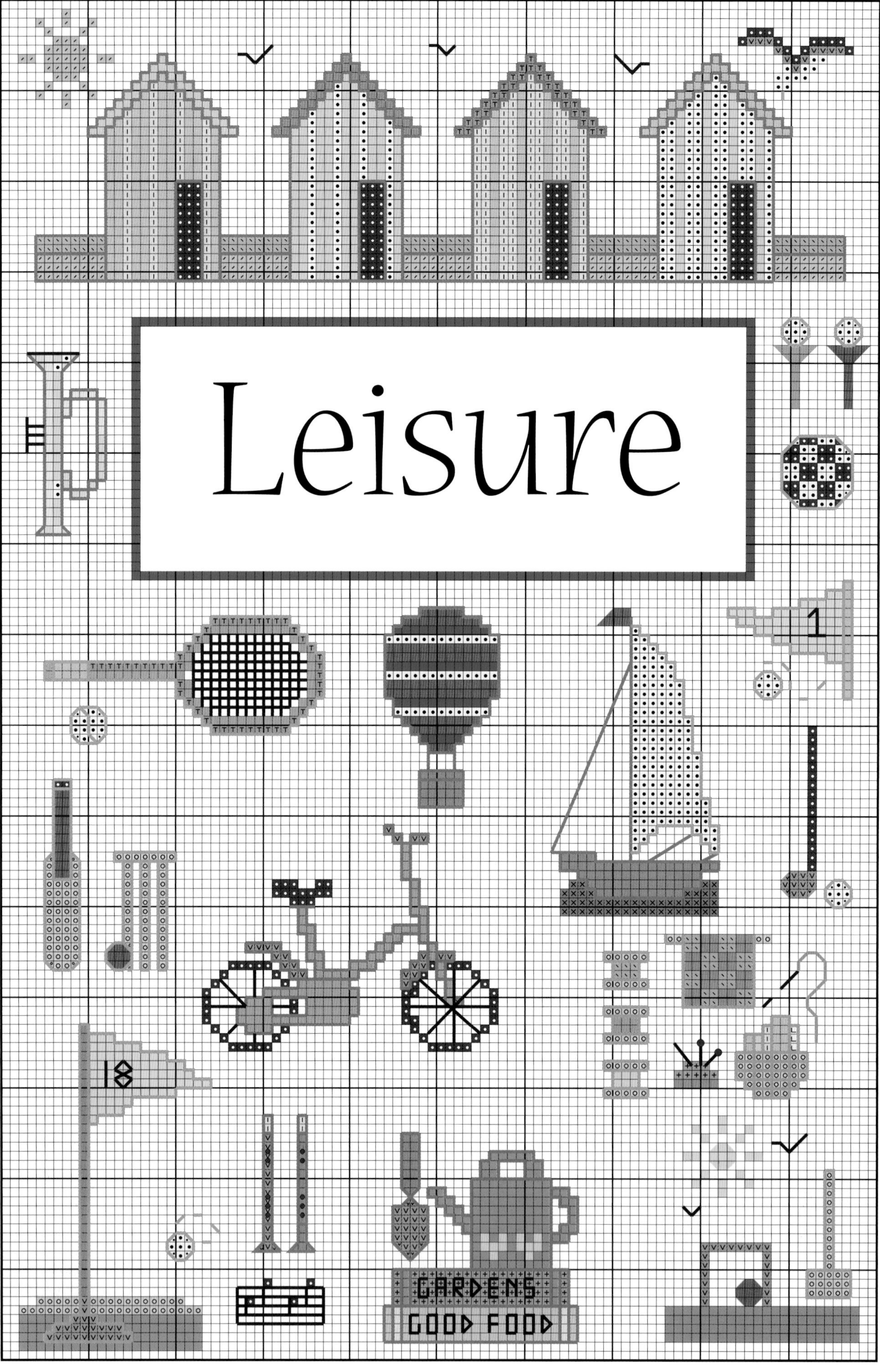
Leisure
1
18
GARDENS
GOOD FOOD

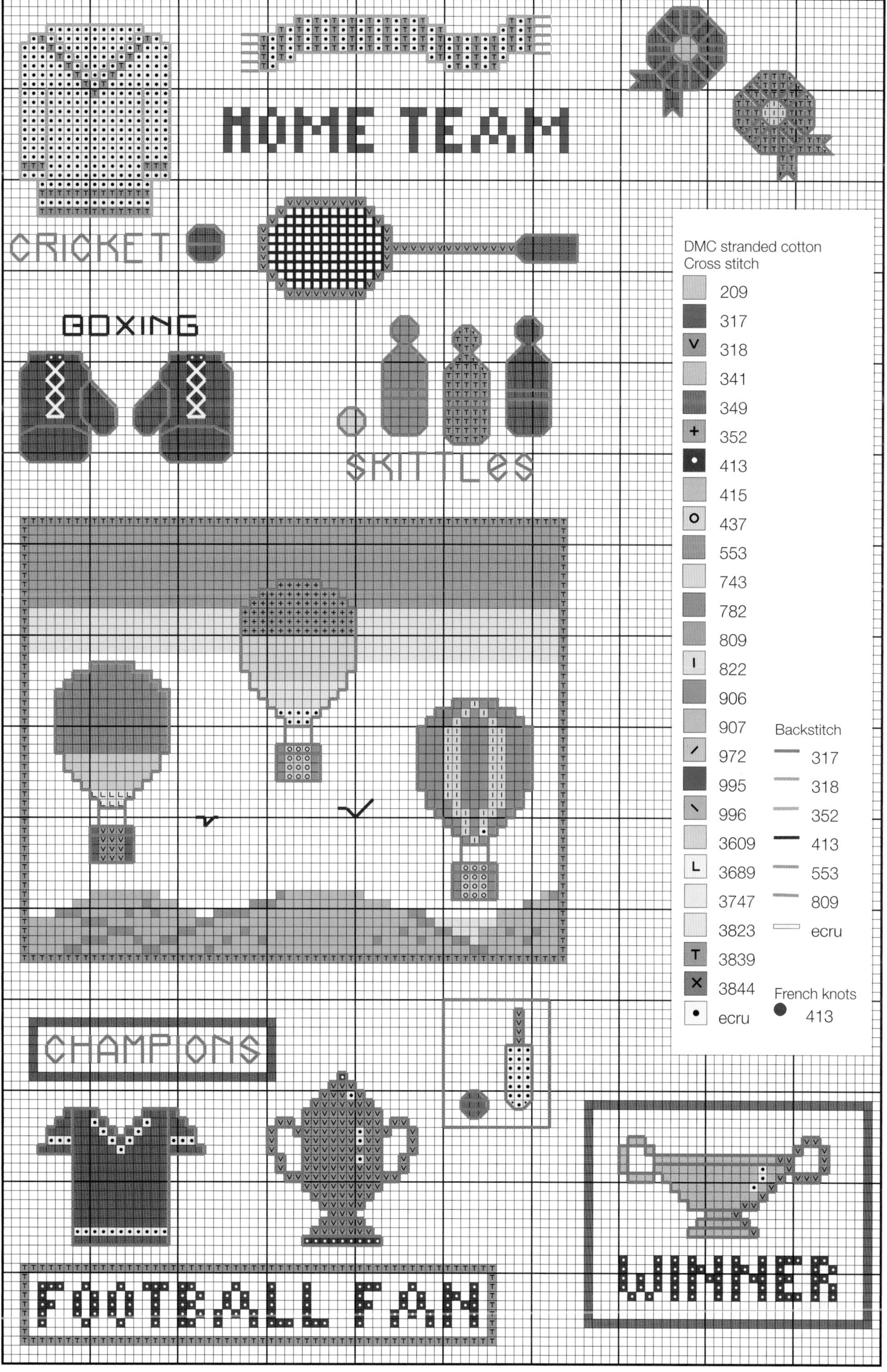
HOME TEAM
CRICKET
BOXING
SKITTLES
CHAMPIONS
FOOTBALL FAN
WINNER
DMC stranded cotton
Cross stitch
209
317
V 318
341
349
+ 352
• 413
415
O 437
553
743
782
809
I 822
906
907
/ 972
995
\ 996
3609
L 3689
3747
3823
T 3839
X 3844
• ecru
Backstitch
317
318
352
413
553
809
ecru
French knots
413

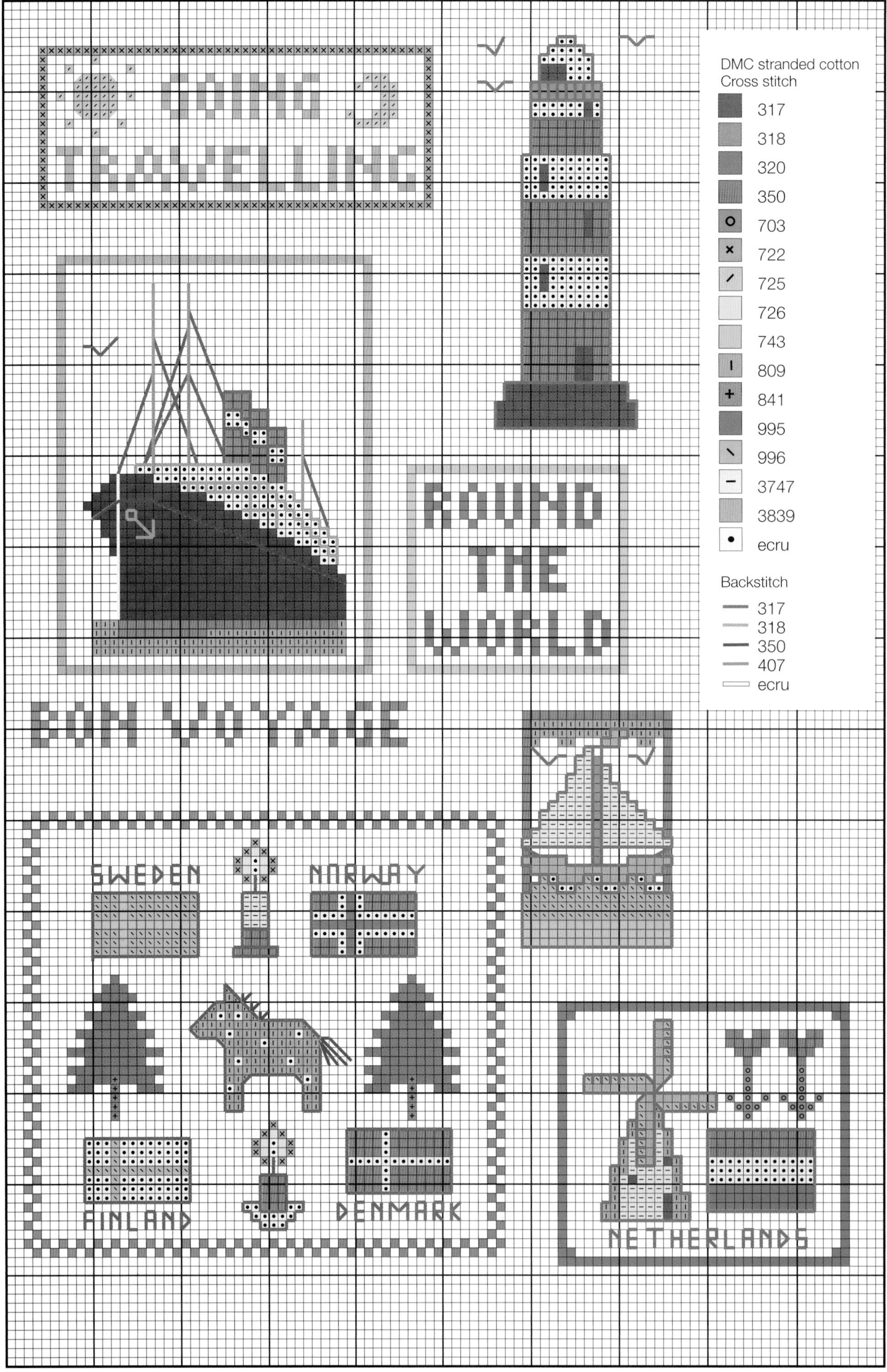
GOING TRAVELLING
ROUND THE WORLD
BON VOYAGE
SWEDEN
NORWAY
FINLAND
DENMARK
NETHERLANDS
DMC stranded cotton
Cross stitch
317
318
320
350
703
722
725
726
743
809
841
995
996
3747
3839
ecru
Backstitch
317
318
350
407
ecru

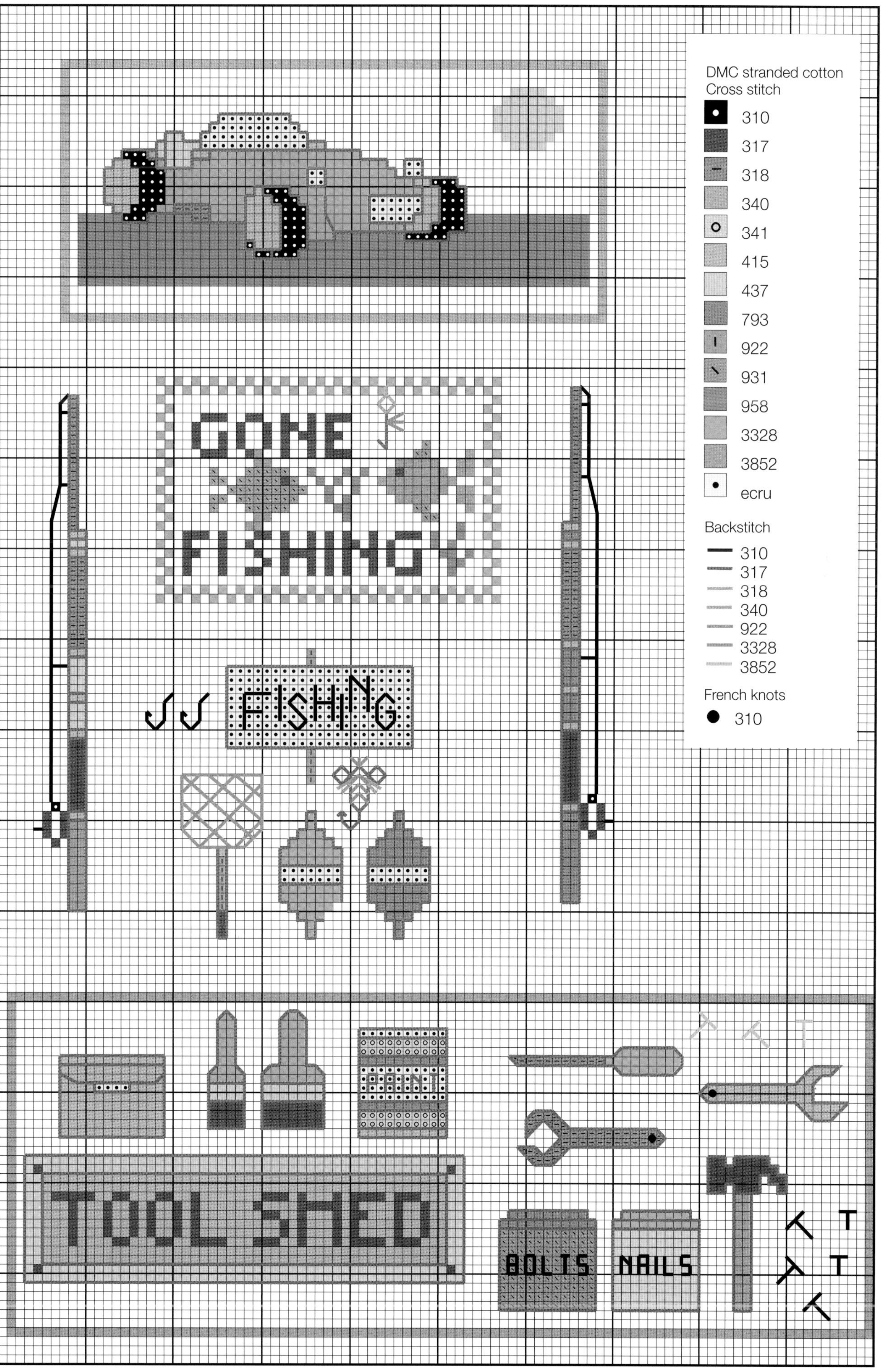
GONE
FISHING
FISHING
TOOL SHED
BOLTS
NAILS
DMC stranded cotton
Cross stitch
310
317
318
340
341
415
437
793
922
931
958
3328
3852
ecru
Backstitch
310
317
318
340
922
3328
3852
French knots
310

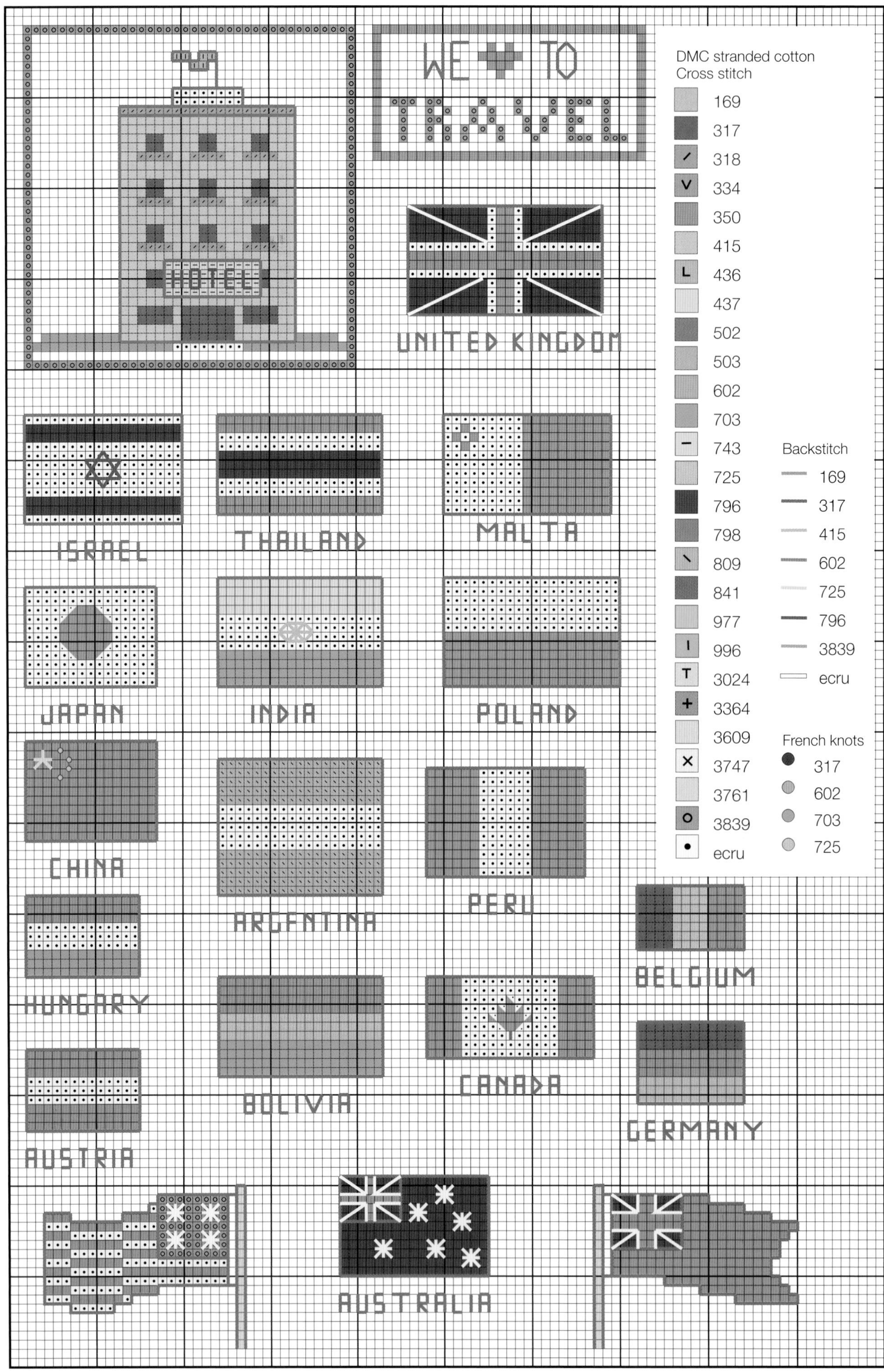
WE ♥ TO
TRAVEL
HOTEL
UNITED KINGDOM
ISRAEL
THAILAND
MALTA
JAPAN
INDIA
POLAND
CHINA
ARGENTINA
PERU
BELGIUM
HUNGARY
BOLIVIA
CANADA
GERMANY
AUSTRIA
AUSTRALIA
DMC stranded cotton
Cross stitch
169
317
318
334
350
415
436
437
502
503
602
703
743
725
796
798
809
841
977
996
3024
3364
3609
3747
3761
3839
ecru
Backstitch
169
317
415
602
725
796
3839
ecru
French knots
317
602
703
725

Leisure Motifs

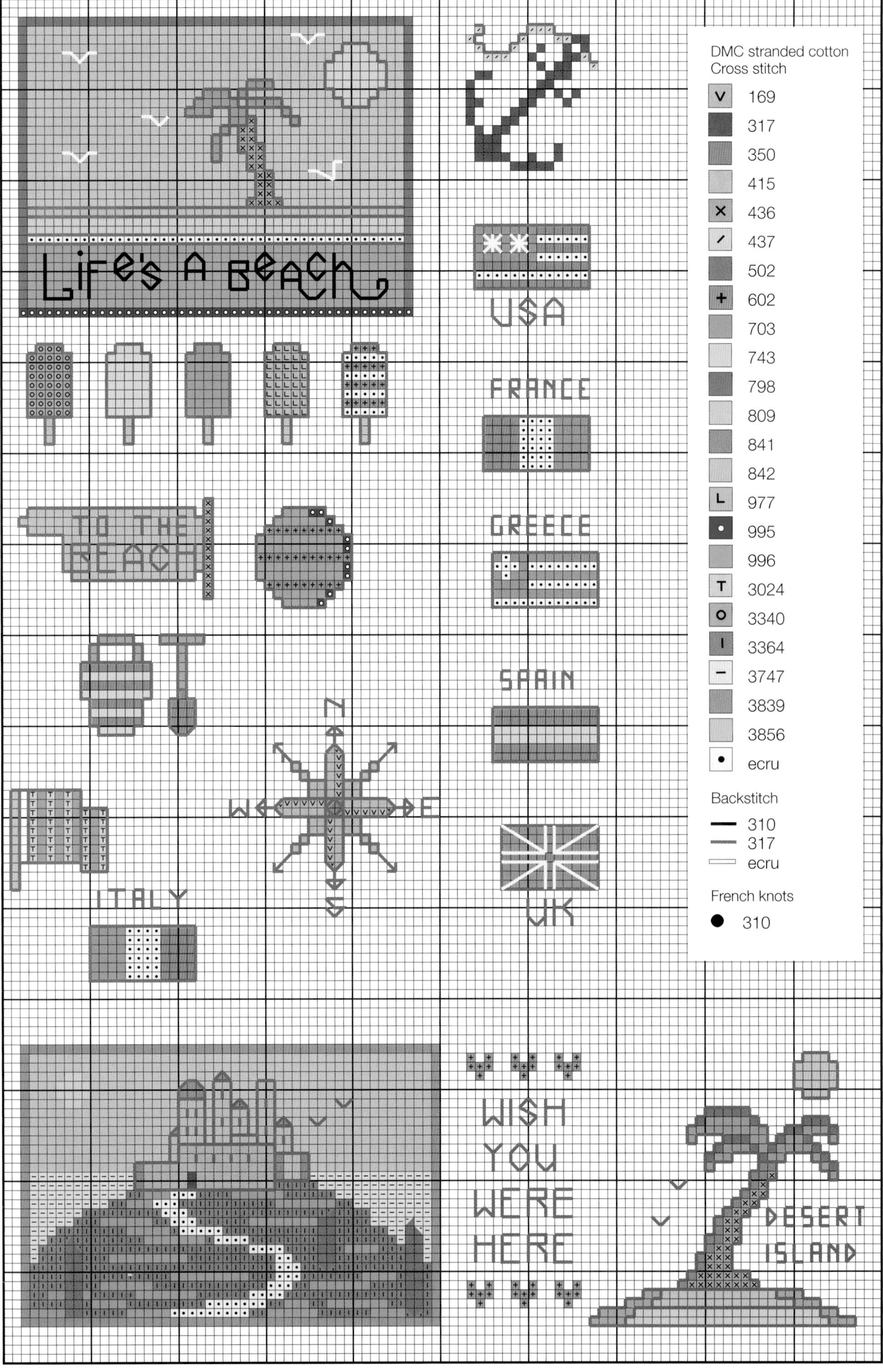
LIFE'S A BEACH
USA
FRANCE
GREECE
SPAIN
UK
TO THE BEACH
ITALY
N
S
W
E
WISH YOU WERE HERE
DESERT ISLAND
DMC stranded cotton
Cross stitch
169
317
350
415
436
437
502
602
703
743
798
809
841
842
977
995
996
3024
3340
3364
3747
3839
3856
ecru
Backstitch
310
317
ecru
French knots
310

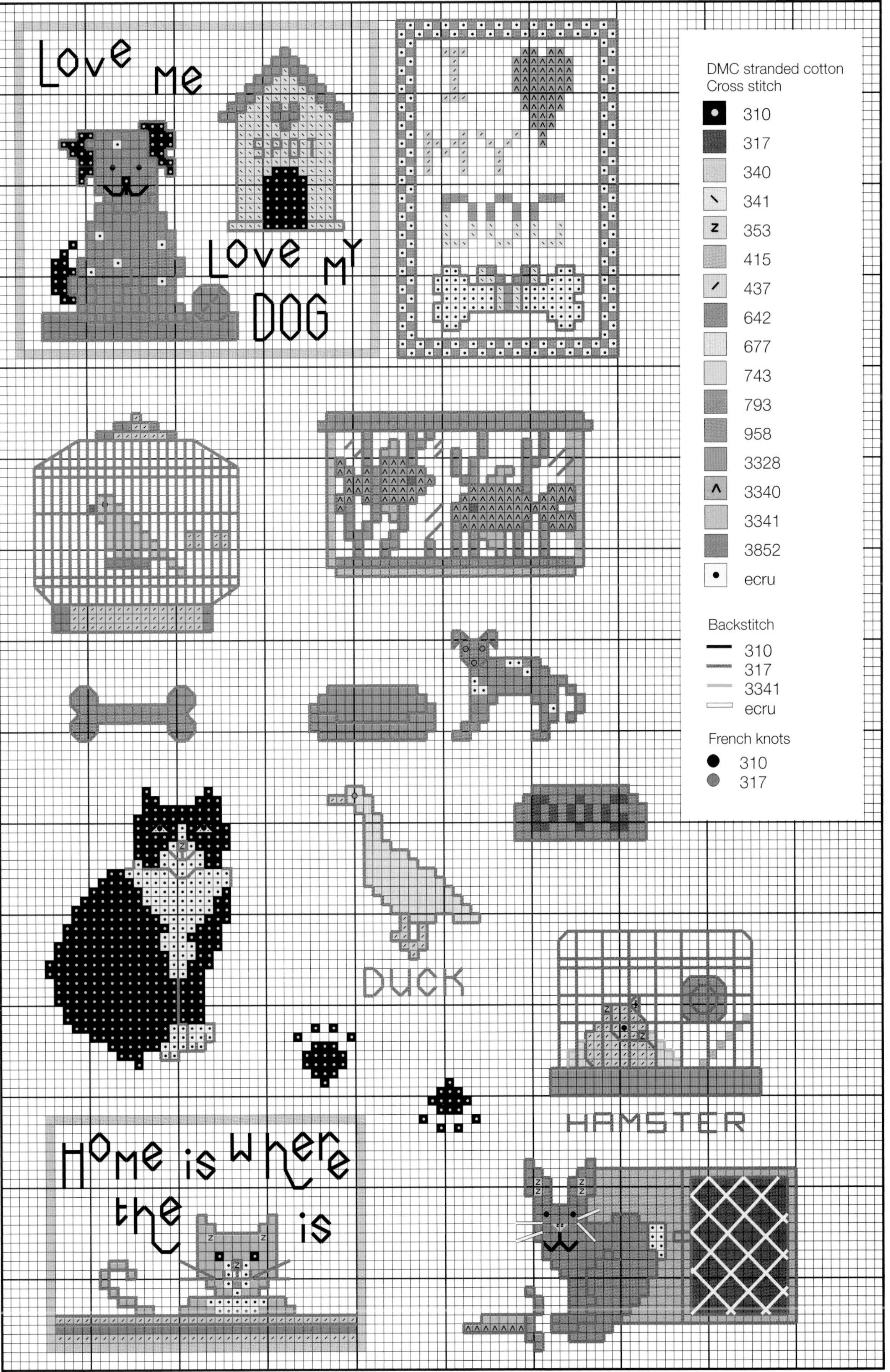

Love me
Love my
DOG
DOG
DUCK
HAMSTER
Home is where
the
is
DMC stranded cotton
Cross stitch
310
317
340
341
353
415
437
642
677
743
793
958
3328
3340
3341
3852
ecru
Backstitch
310
317
3341
ecru
French knots
310
317

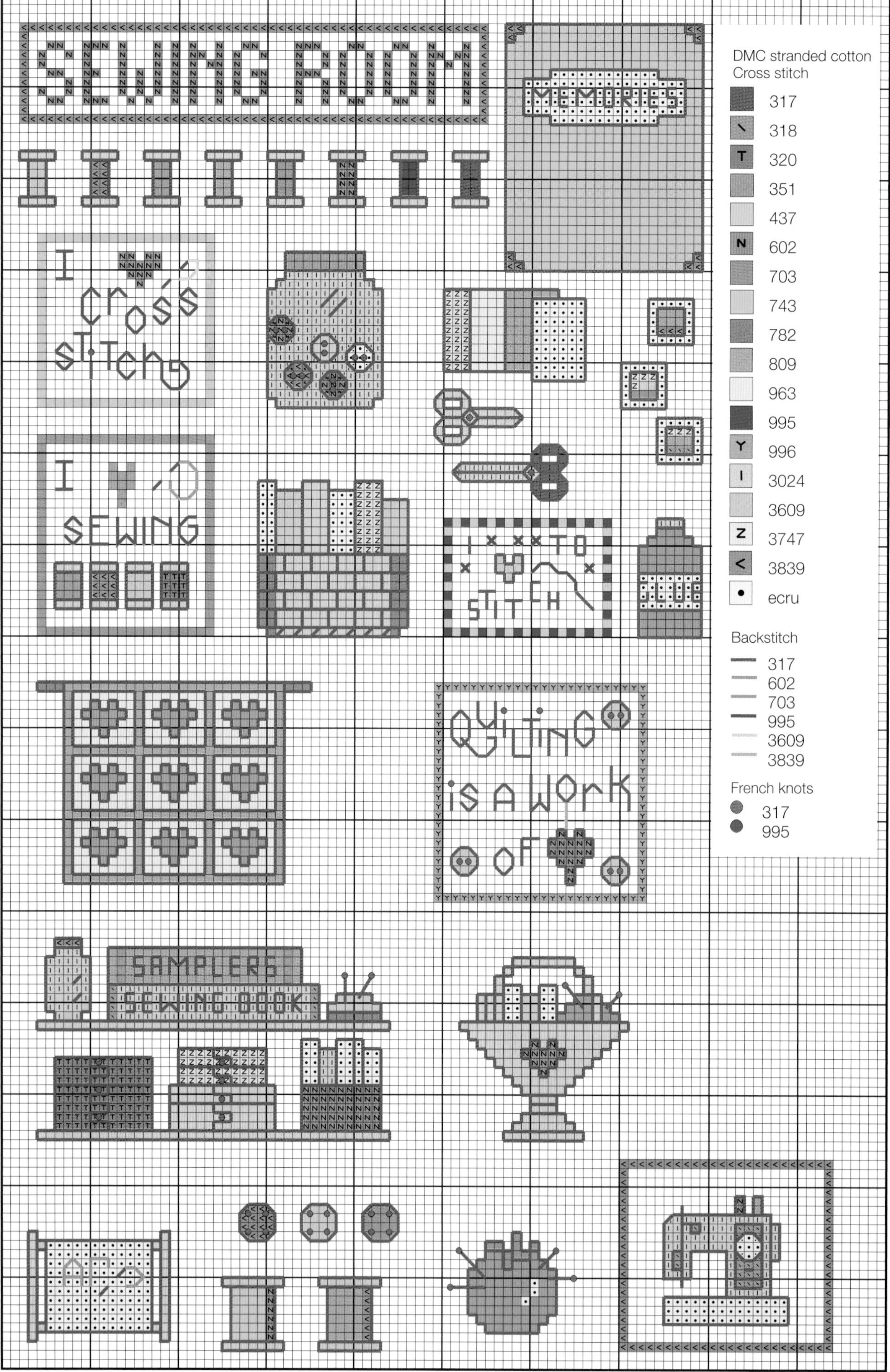
SEWING ROOM
MEMORIES
I cross stitch
I SEWING
SAMPLERS
SEWING BOOK
I TO STITCH
QUILTING is a WORK of
DMC stranded cotton
Cross stitch
317
318
320
351
437
602
703
743
782
809
963
995
996
3024
3609
3747
3839
ecru
Backstitch
317
602
703
995
3609
3839
French knots
317
995

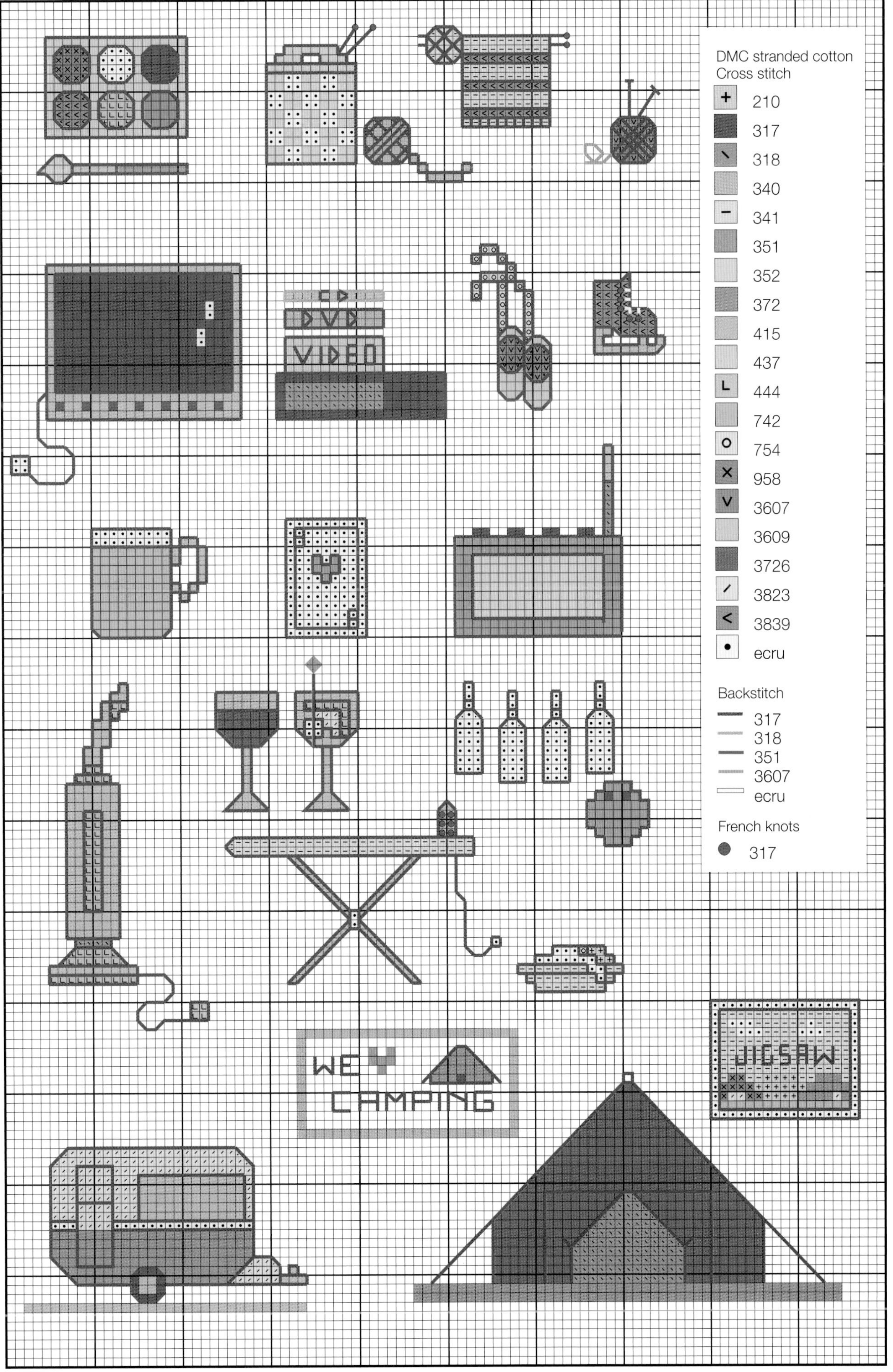
DMC stranded cotton
Cross stitch
+ 210
317
318
340
341
351
352
372
415
437
L 444
742
o 754
× 958
V 3607
3609
3726
3823
< 3839
• ecru
Backstitch
317
318
351
3607
ecru
French knots
317
VIDEO
WE
CAMPING
JIGSAW

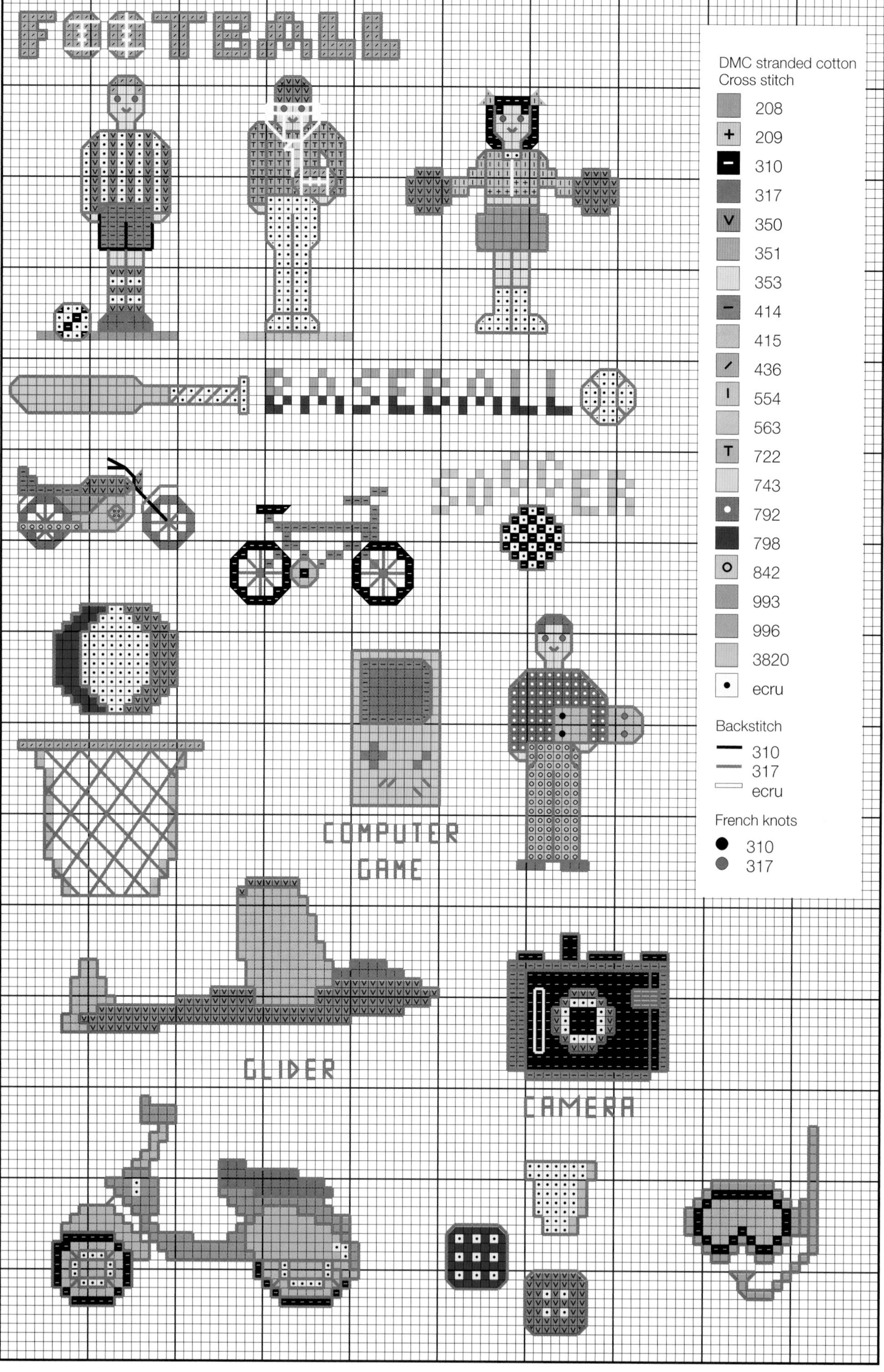
FOOTBALL
BASEBALL
SOCCER
COMPUTER
GAME
GLIDER
CAMERA
DMC stranded cotton
Cross stitch
208
209
310
317
350
351
353
414
415
436
554
563
722
743
792
798
842
993
996
3820
ecru
Backstitch
310
317
ecru
French knots
310
317

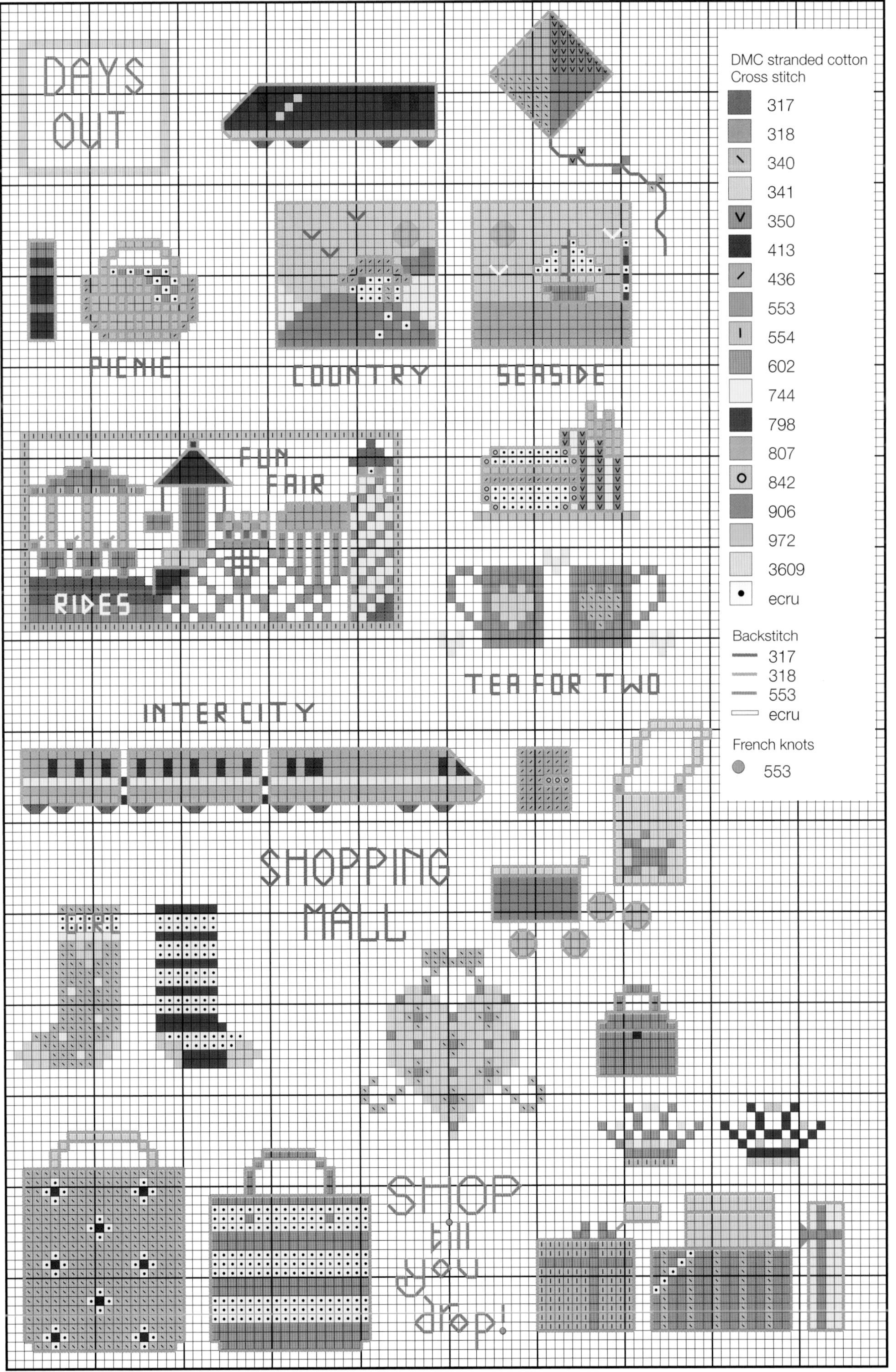
DAYS OUT
PICNIC
COUNTRY
SEASIDE
FUN FAIR
RIDES
TEA FOR TWO
INTER CITY
SHOPPING MALL
SHOP till you drop!
DMC stranded cotton
Cross stitch
317
318
340
341
350
413
436
553
554
602
744
798
807
842
906
972
3609
ecru
Backstitch
317
318
553
ecru
French knots
553

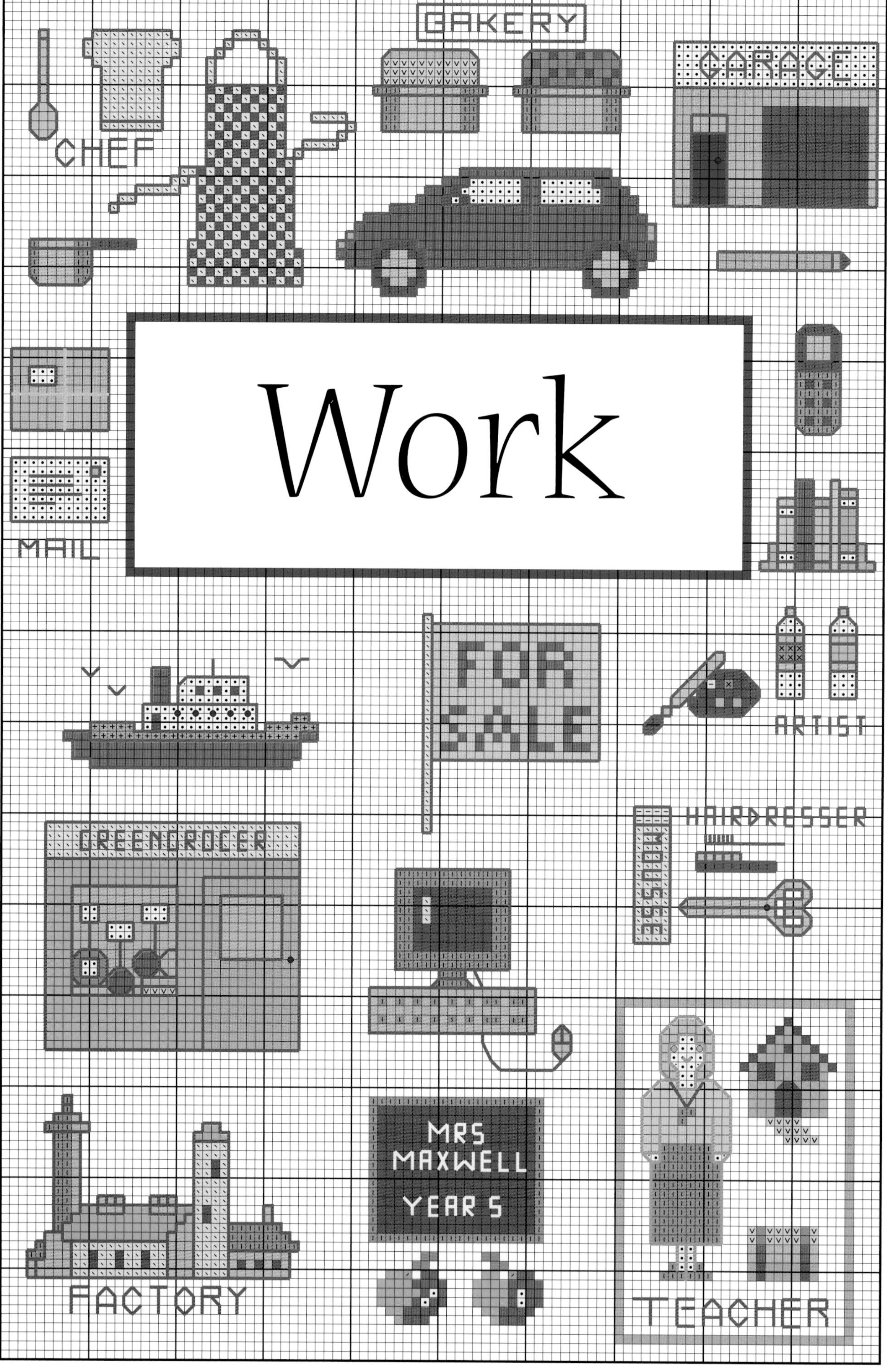
BAKERY
GARAGE
CHEF
Work
MAIL
FOR SALE
ARTIST
HAIRDRESSER
GREENGROCER
MRS
MAXWELL
YEAR 5
FACTORY
TEACHER

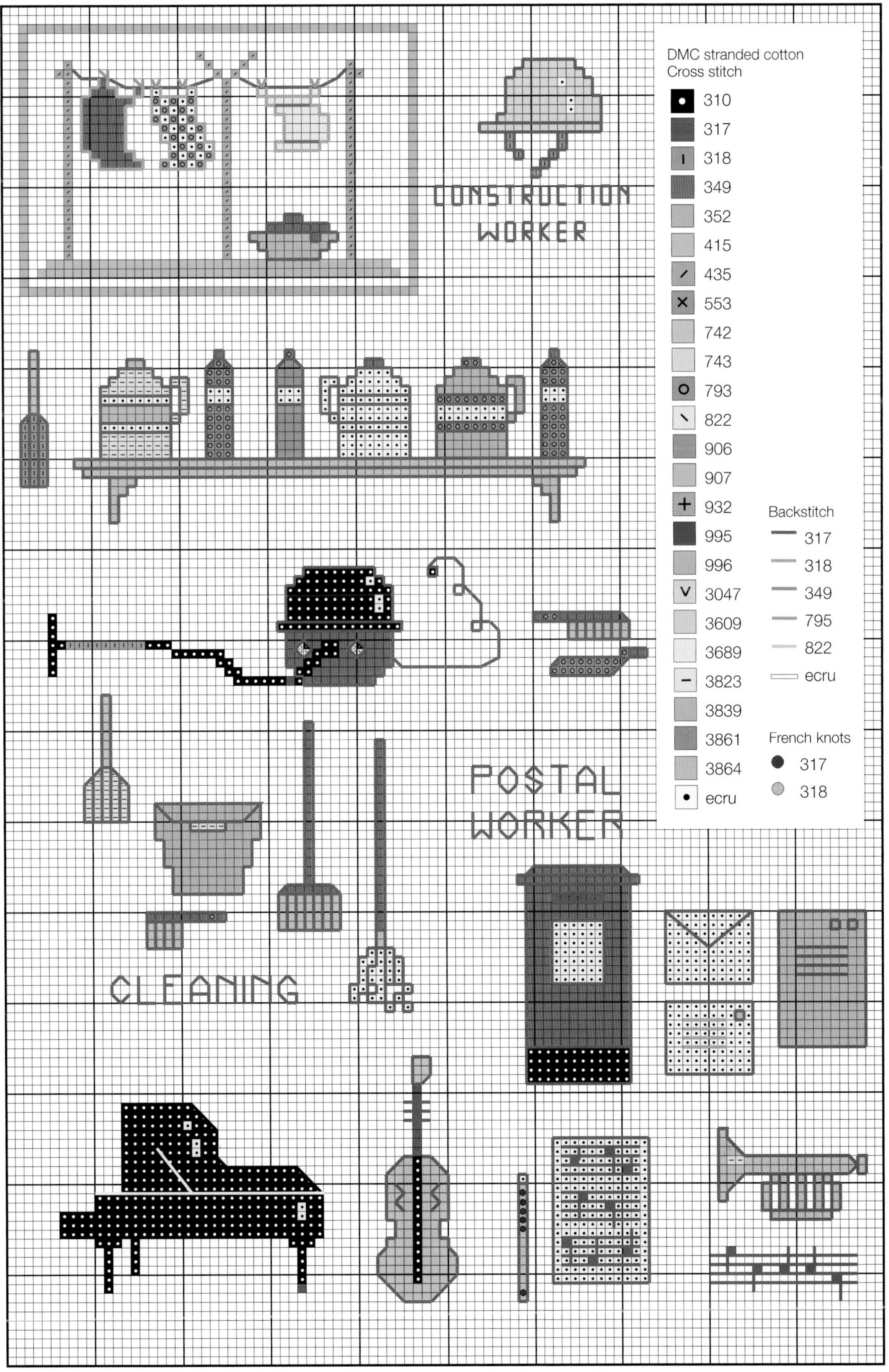
CONSTRUCTION WORKER
POSTAL WORKER
CLEANING
DMC stranded cotton
Cross stitch
310
317
318
349
352
415
435
553
742
743
793
822
906
907
932
995
996
3047
3609
3689
3823
3839
3861
3864
ecru
Backstitch
317
318
349
795
822
ecru
French knots
317
318

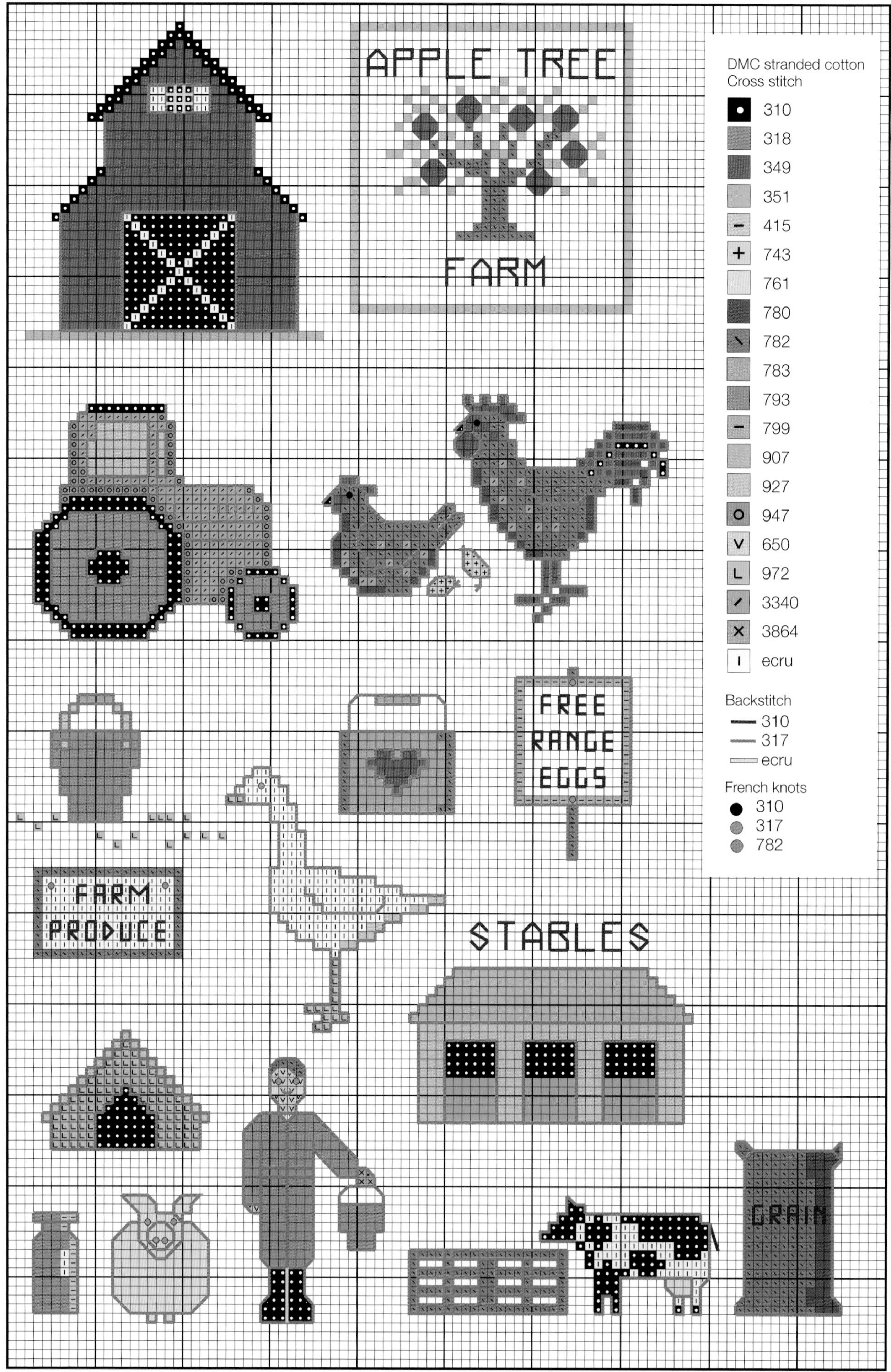
APPLE TREE
FARM
FREE
RANGE
EGGS
FARM
PRODUCE
STABLES
GRAIN
DMC stranded cotton
Cross stitch
310
318
349
351
415
743
761
780
782
783
793
799
907
927
947
650
972
3340
3864
ecru
Backstitch
310
317
ecru
French knots
310
317
782

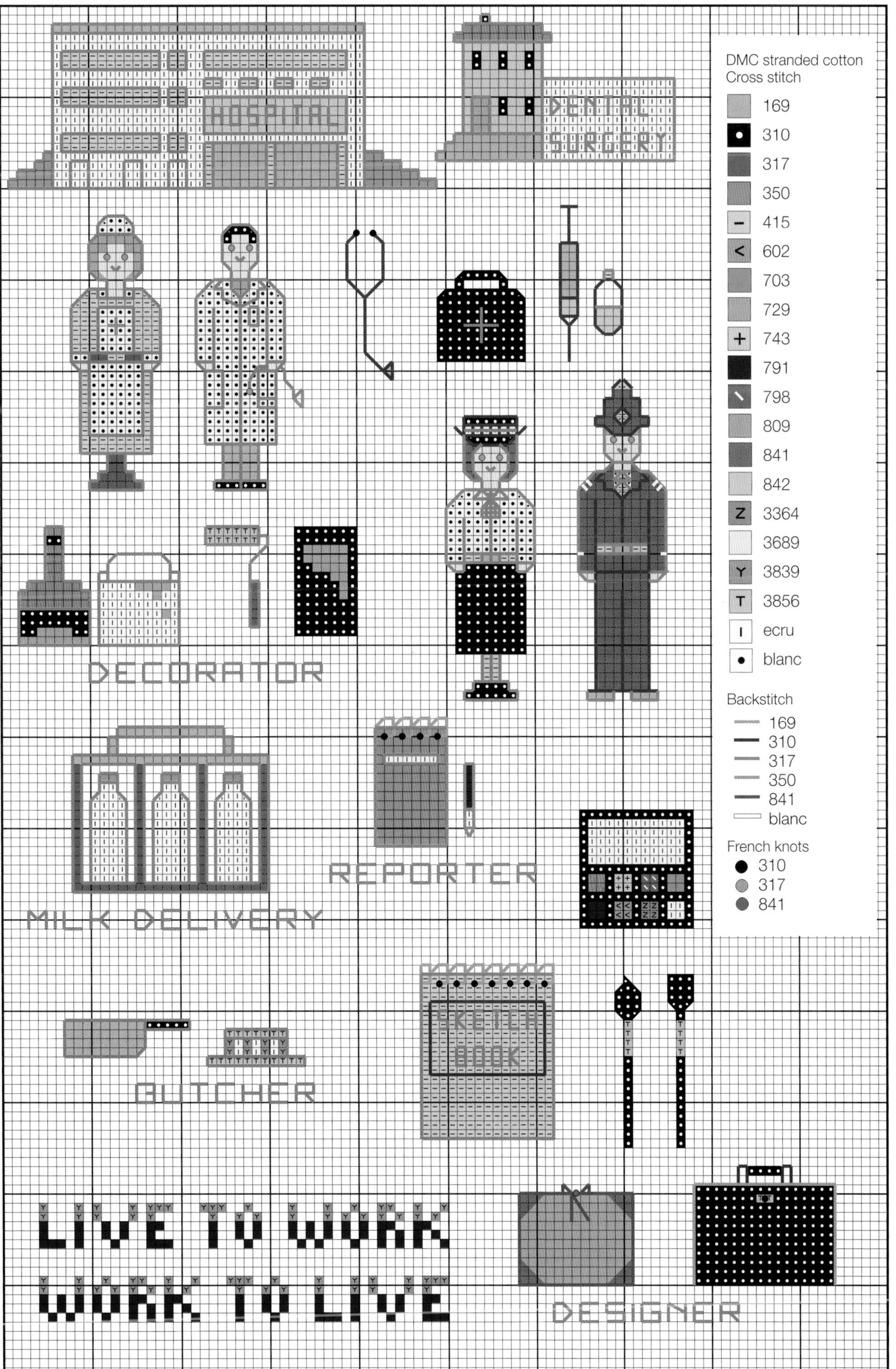
HOSPITAL
DENTAL SURGERY
DECORATOR
REPORTER
MILK DELIVERY
SKETCH BOOK
BUTCHER
LIVE TO WORK
WORK TO LIVE
DESIGNER
DMC stranded cotton
Cross stitch
169
310
317
350
415
602
703
729
743
791
798
809
841
842
3364
3689
3839
3856
ecru
blanc
Backstitch
169
310
317
350
841
blanc
French knots
310
317
841

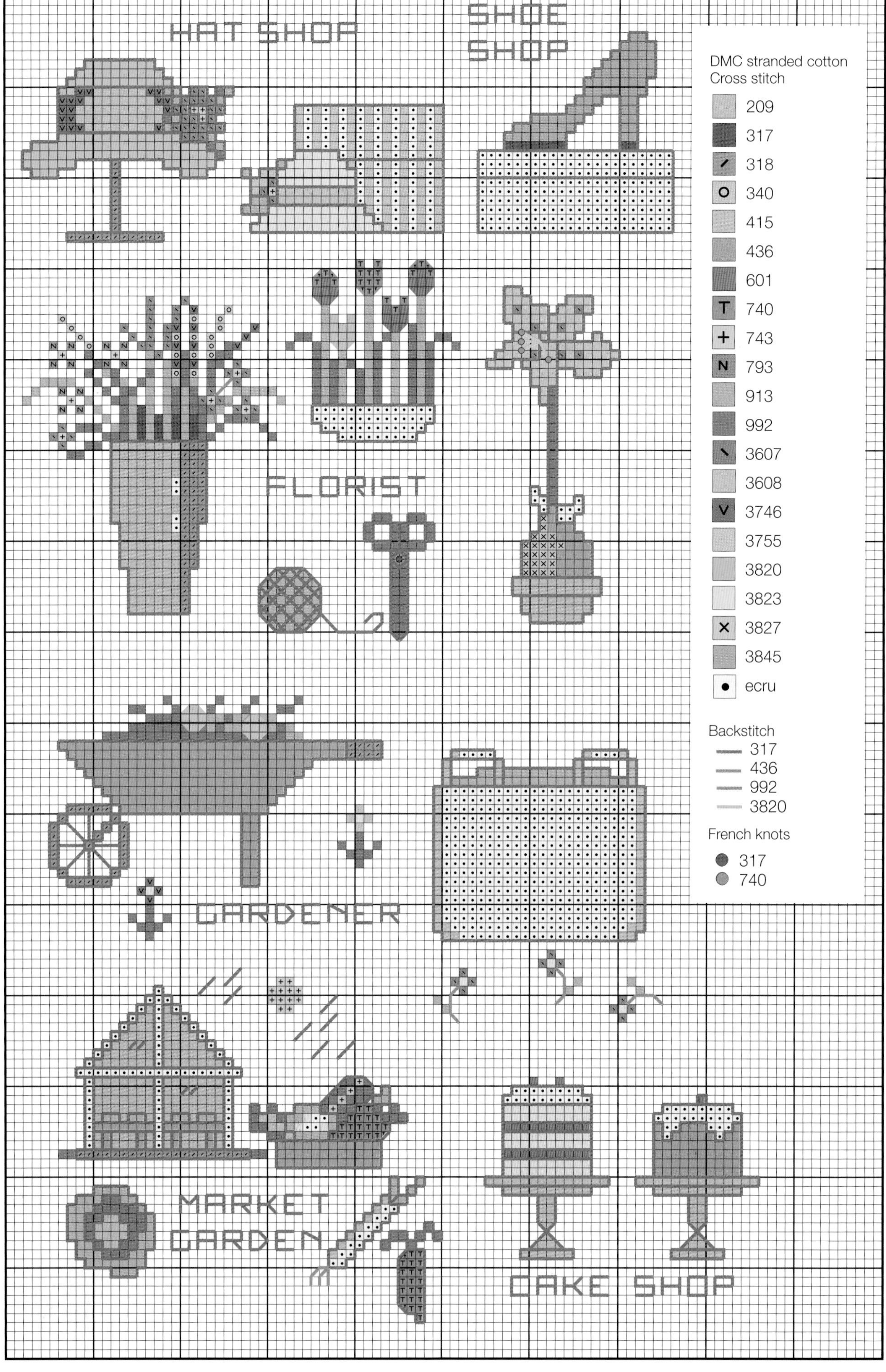
HAT SHOP
SHOE SHOP
FLORIST
GARDENER
MARKET GARDEN
CAKE SHOP
DMC stranded cotton
Cross stitch
209
317
318
340
415
436
601
740
743
793
913
992
3607
3608
3746
3755
3820
3823
3827
3845
ecru
Backstitch
317
436
992
3820
French knots
317
740

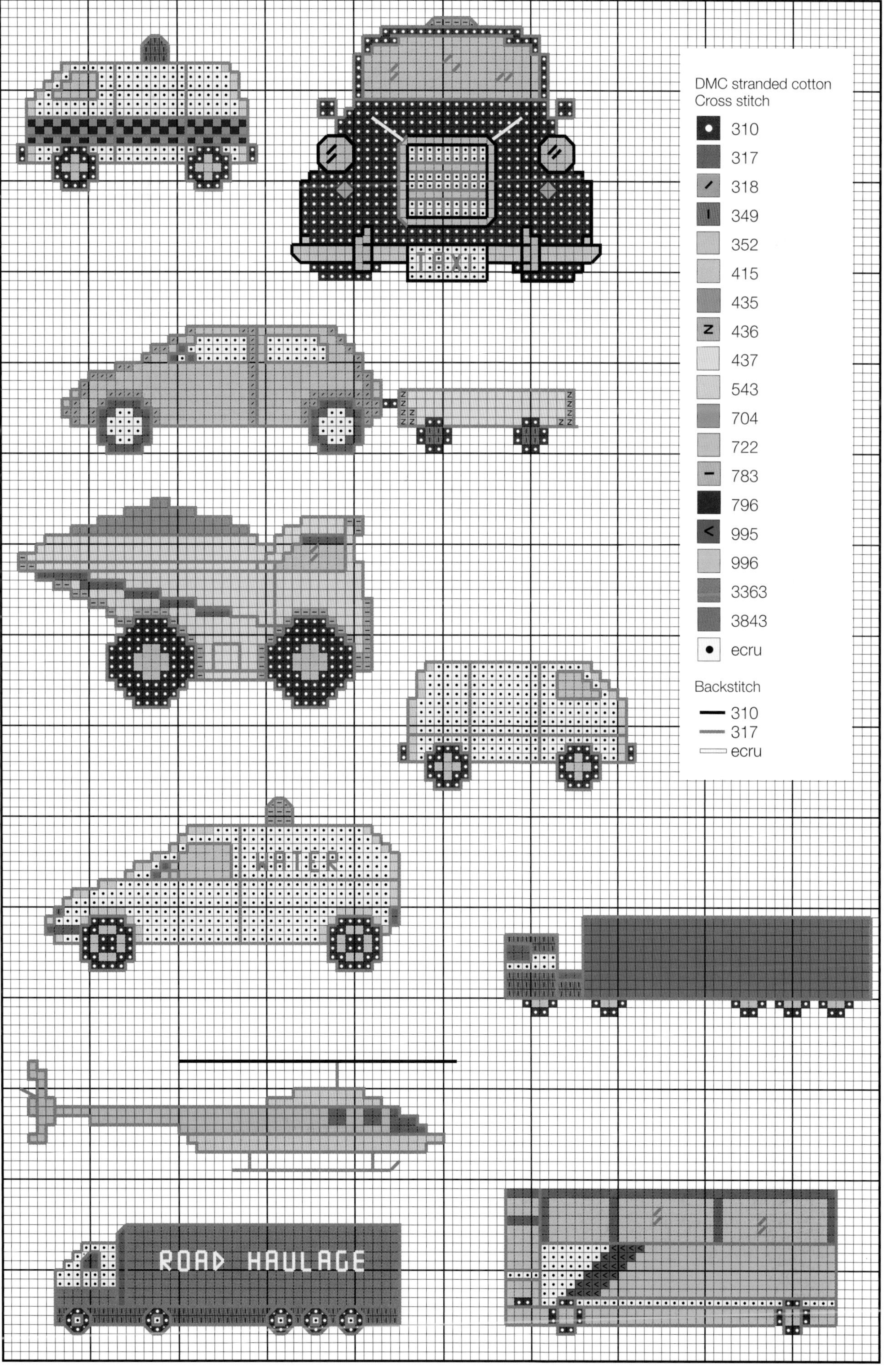
DMC stranded cotton
Cross stitch
310
317
318
349
352
415
435
436
437
543
704
722
783
796
995
996
3363
3843
ecru
Backstitch
310
317
ecru
TAXI
ROAD HAULAGE

Seasons
YOU are
MY
SUNSHINE

DMC stranded cotton
Cross stitch
317
318
349
352
415
435
553
677
799
809
833
906
907
922
972
977
996
3608
3609
3689
3806
3814
3863
ecru
Backstitch
317
799
906
3806
3814
ecru
French knots
317
799
ecru
SWEET SPRING
HONEY
BEES
TALLEST
SUNFLOWER
COMPETITION
Berry Picking

Spring
HAPPY EASTER
EASTER GREETINGS
EASTER
DMC stranded cotton
Cross stitch
209
318
340
341
350
402
413
415
437
472
552
725
741
798
894
906
907
945
3688
3689
3823
blanc
ecru
Backstitch
317
413
502
741
French knots
318
350
blanc

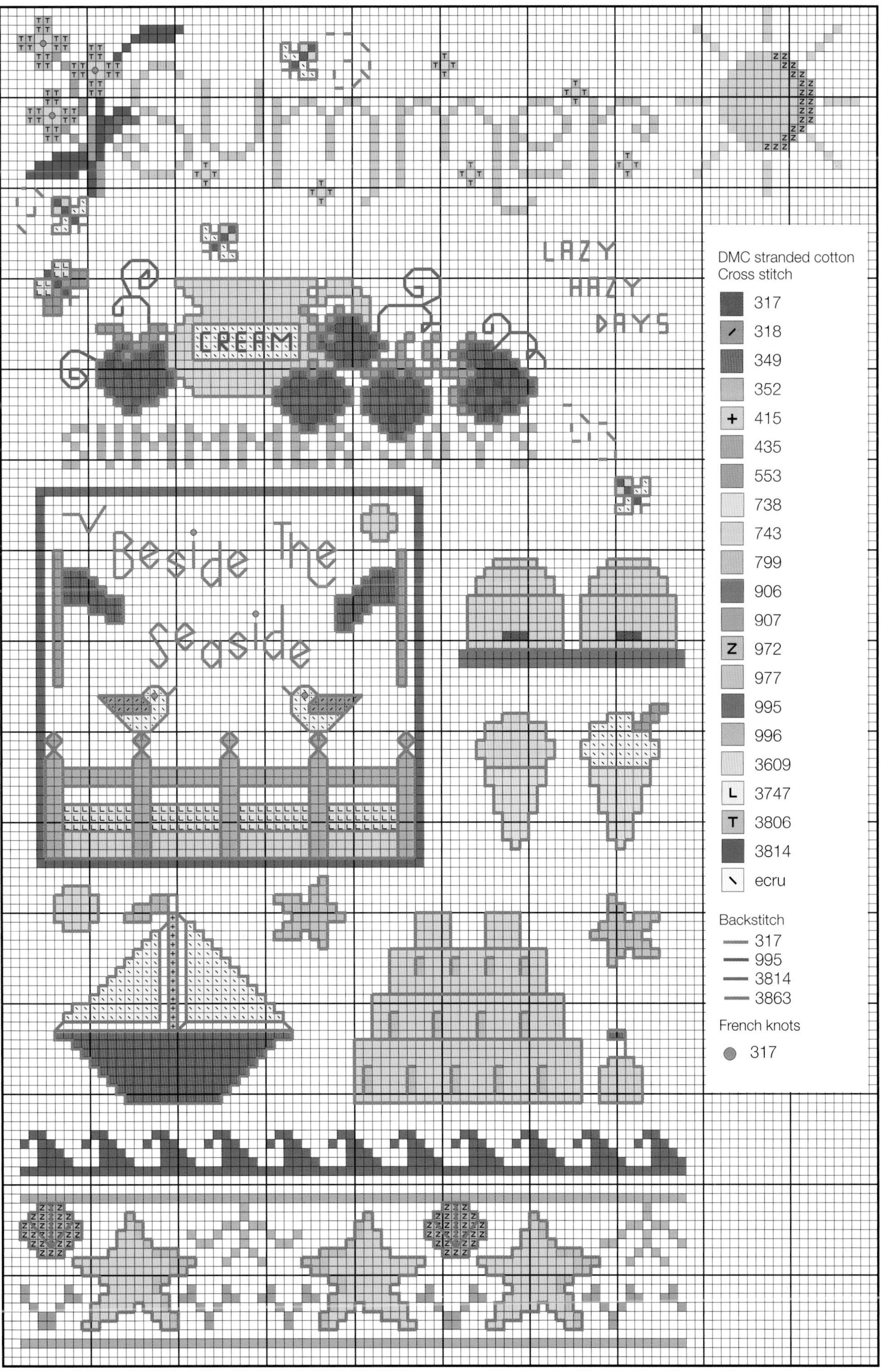
LAZY
HAZY
DAYS
CREAM
Beside The
Seaside
DMC stranded cotton
Cross stitch
317
/ 318
349
352
+ 415
435
553
738
743
799
906
907
Z 972
977
995
996
3609
L 3747
T 3806
3814
\ ecru
Backstitch
317
995
3814
3863
French knots
317

Autumn
season of mists
&
mellow
fruitfulness
VEG BOX
HAPPY Harvest
HAPPY
THANKS GiViNG
Trick or Treat
HAPPY
HALLOWEEN
DMC stranded cotton
Cross stitch
310
317
318
340
350
351
353
402
415
435
436
502
552
725
741
809
906
907
921
3823
ecru
Backstitch
310
317
435
502
552
906
921
ecru
French knots
317
925

DMC stranded cotton
Cross stitch
209
× 340
+ 351
413
I 436
726
740
o 793
825
840
Y 932
992
996
T 3042
3325
3608
3779
L 3804
< 3820
3823
/ blanc
• ecru
Backstitch
317
413
932
992
3820
French knots
● 413

VALENTINE
HAPPY
EASTER
WISHING YOU
GOOD
LUCK
JULY
4
FROM SEA
TO
SEA
SHINING
HAPPY
THANKSGIVING
CORN
WHEAT
FLOUR
DMC stranded cotton
Cross stitch
223
310
317
318
350
415
553
743
744
799
825
906
907
922
972
977
995
3608
3609
3814
3861
ecru
Backstitch
310
317
977
3814
ecru
French knots
317

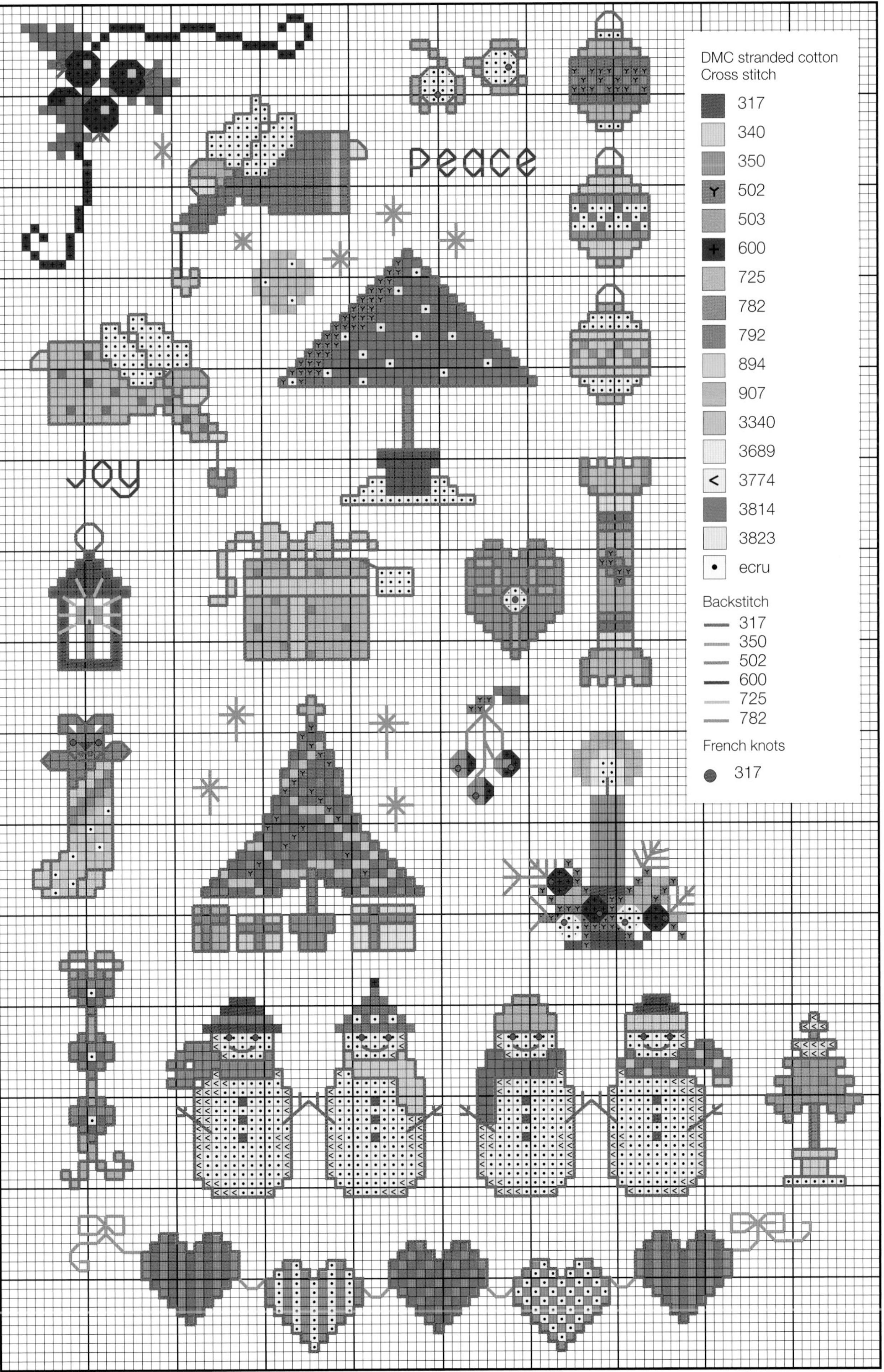
Peace
Joy
DMC stranded cotton
Cross stitch
317
340
350
502
503
600
725
782
792
894
907
3340
3689
3774
3814
3823
ecru
Backstitch
317
350
502
600
725
782
French knots
317

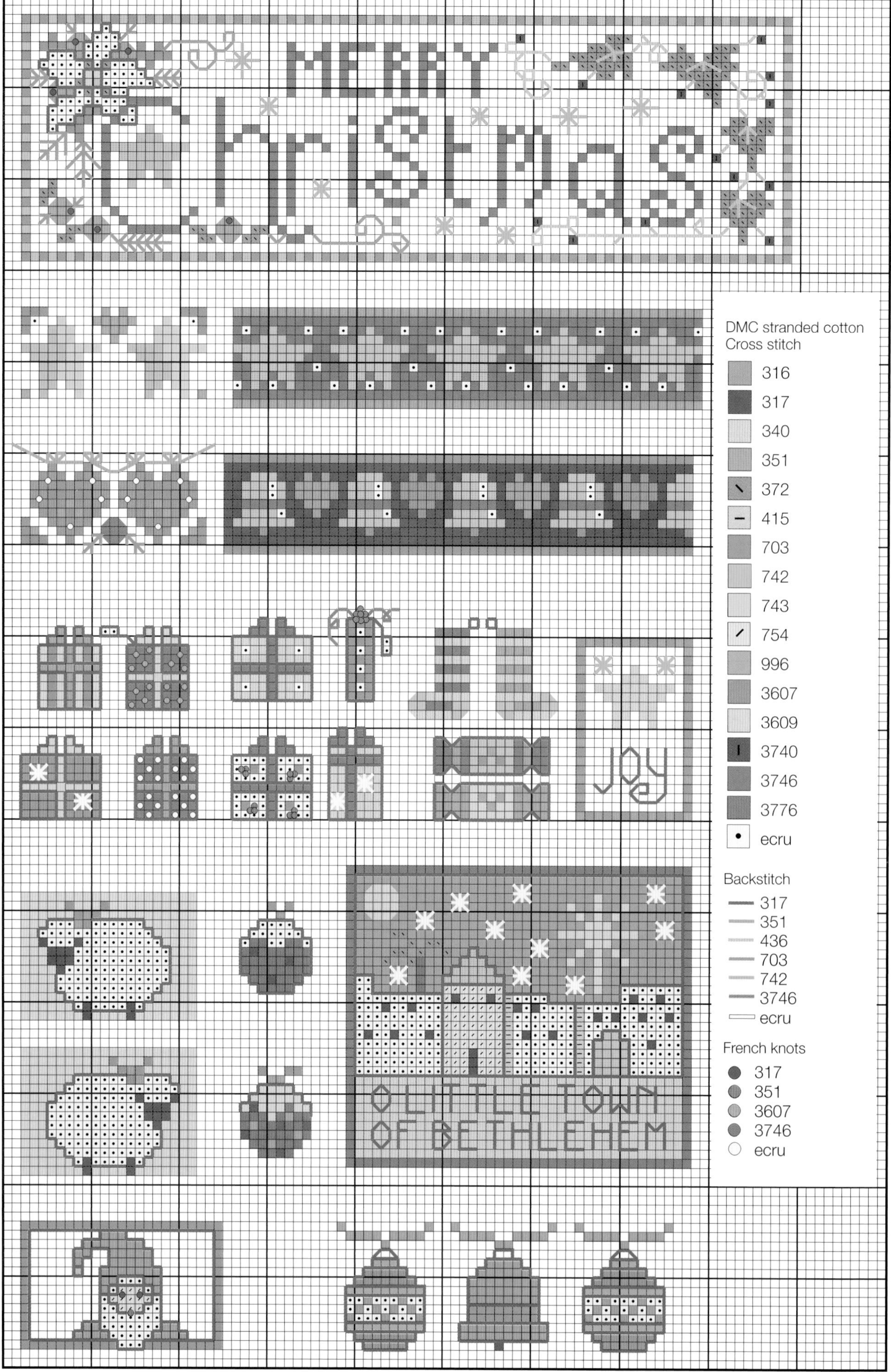
MERRY
Christmas
JOY
O LITTLE TOWN
OF BETHLEHEM
DMC stranded cotton
Cross stitch
316
317
340
351
372
415
703
742
743
754
996
3607
3609
3740
3746
3776
ecru
Backstitch
317
351
436
703
742
3746
ecru
French knots
317
351
3607
3746
ecru

DMC stranded cotton
Cross stitch
310
317
340
351
415
703
742
754
3354
3609
3746
ecru
Backstitch
310
317
351
742
3746
ecru
French knots
310
317
351

ALL HEARTS COME HOME AT CHRISTMAS
MY first CHRISTMAS
MERRY CHRISTMAS
DMC stranded cotton
Cross stitch
310
340
347
349
351
434
436
523
703
742
754
905
972
3354
3607
3609
3746
blanc
ecru
Backstitch
310
317
349
blanc
French knots
310
317

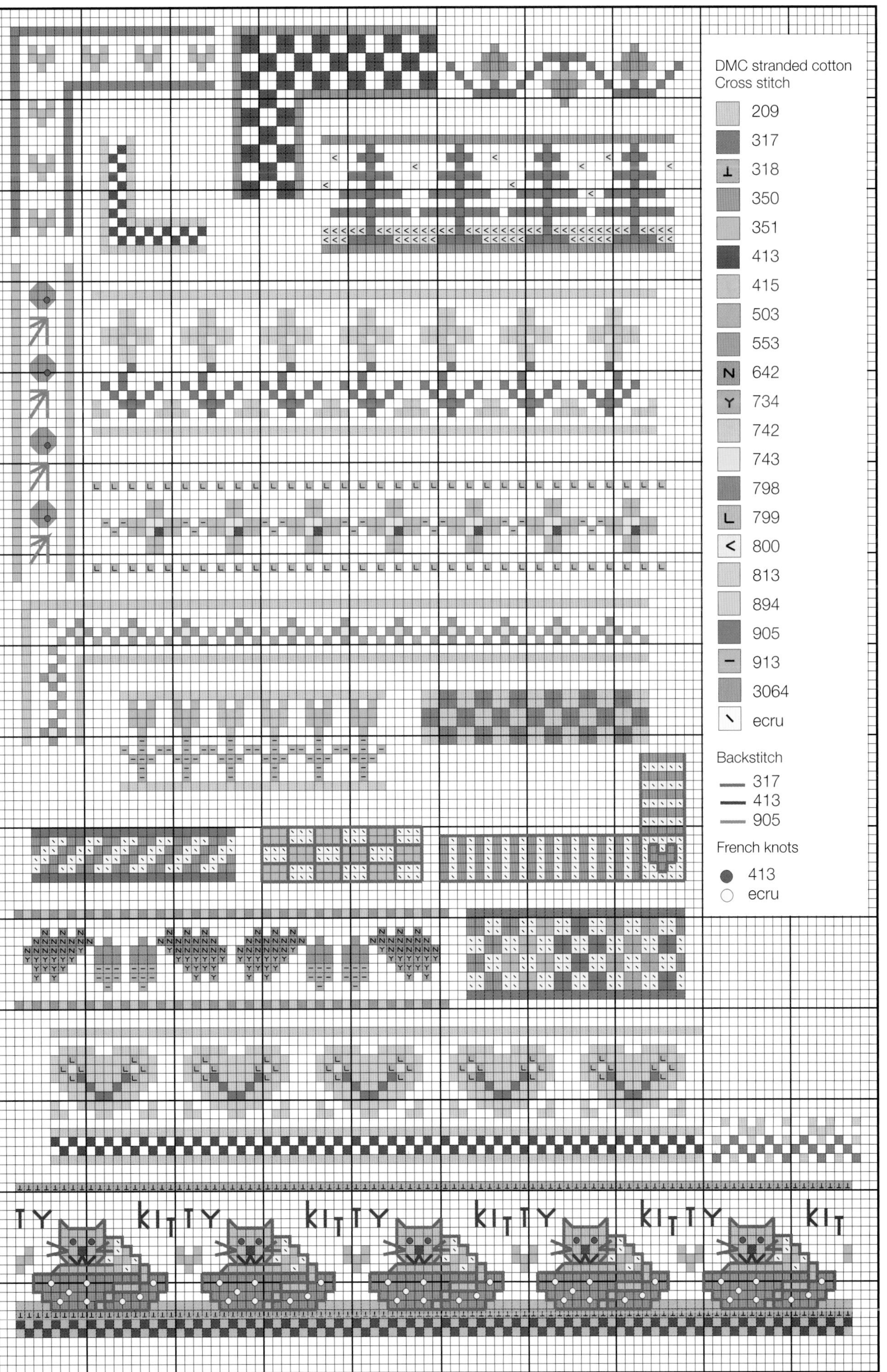
DMC stranded cotton
Cross stitch
209
317
318
350
351
413
415
503
553
642
734
742
743
798
799
800
813
894
905
913
3064
ecru
Backstitch
317
413
905
French knots
413
ecru

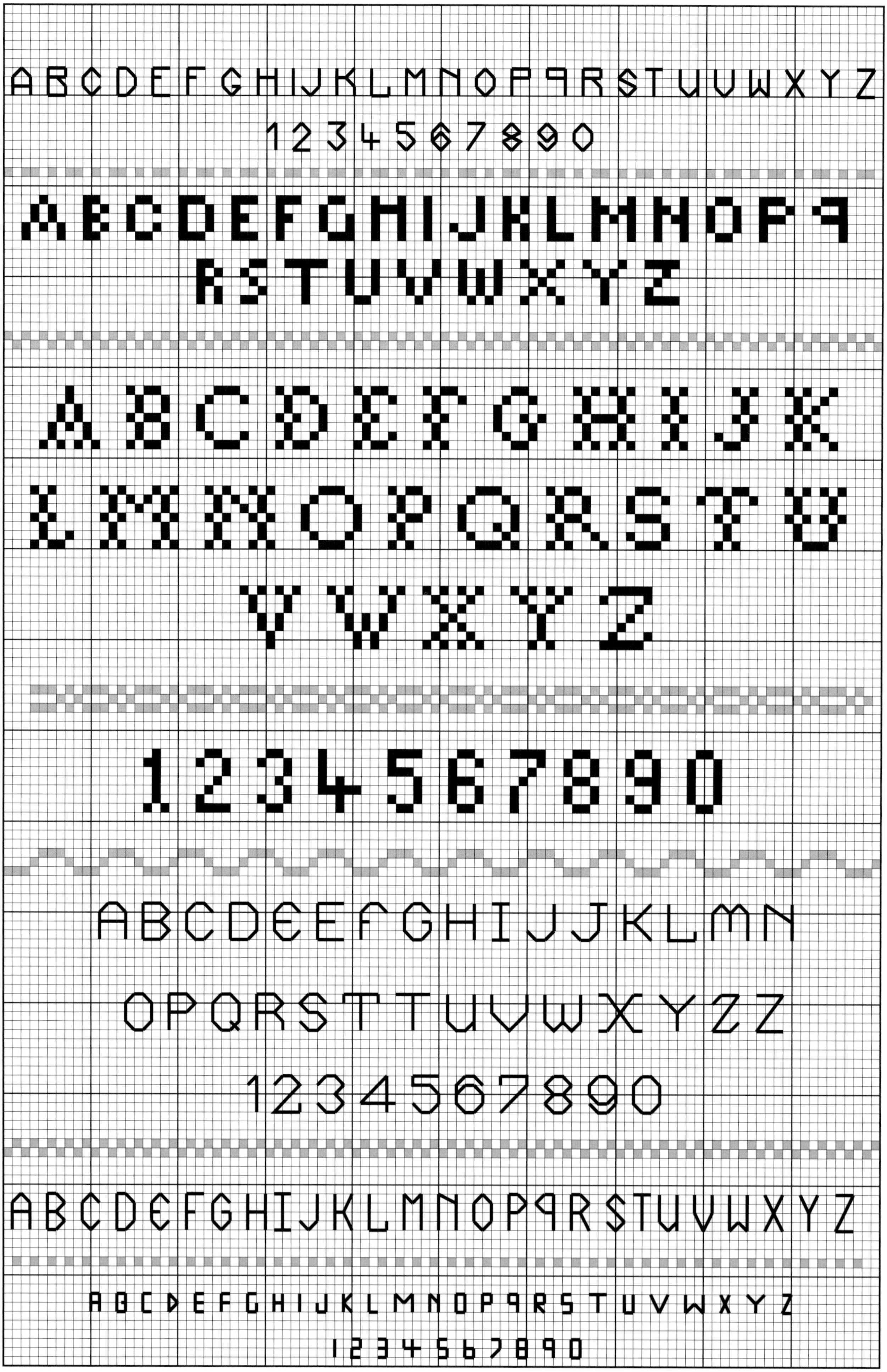

A B C D E F G H I J K L M N O P Q R S T U V W X Y Z

1 2 3 4 5 6 7 8 9 0

A B C D E F G H I J K L M N O P Q

R S T U V W X Y Z

A B C D E F G H I J K

L M N O P Q R S T U

V W X Y Z

1 2 3 4 5 6 7 8 9 0

A B C D E E F G H I J J K L M N

O P Q R S T T U V W X Y Z Z

1 2 3 4 5 6 7 8 9 0

A B C D E F G H I J K L M N O P Q R S T U V W X Y Z

A B C D E F G H I J K L M N O P Q R S T U V W X Y Z

1 2 3 4 5 6 7 8 9 0

a b c d e f g h i j k l m n o p q r s t u v w x y z

1 2 3 4 5 6 7 8 9 0

A B C D E F G H I J K L M
N O P Q R S T U V W
X Y Z

a b c d e f g h i j k l m n o
p q r s t u v w x y z

A B C D E F G H I J K L M N O P Q R S T U V
W X Y Z 1 2 3 4 5 6 7 8 9 0

A B C D E F G H I J K L M N O
P Q R S T U V W X Y Z

1 2 3 4 5 6 7 8 9 0

The Eight Sampler Templates

♥ Template 1 – Nine Patch

Used for the Happy Anniversary sampler on page 8
(Stitch count: 75h x 75w)

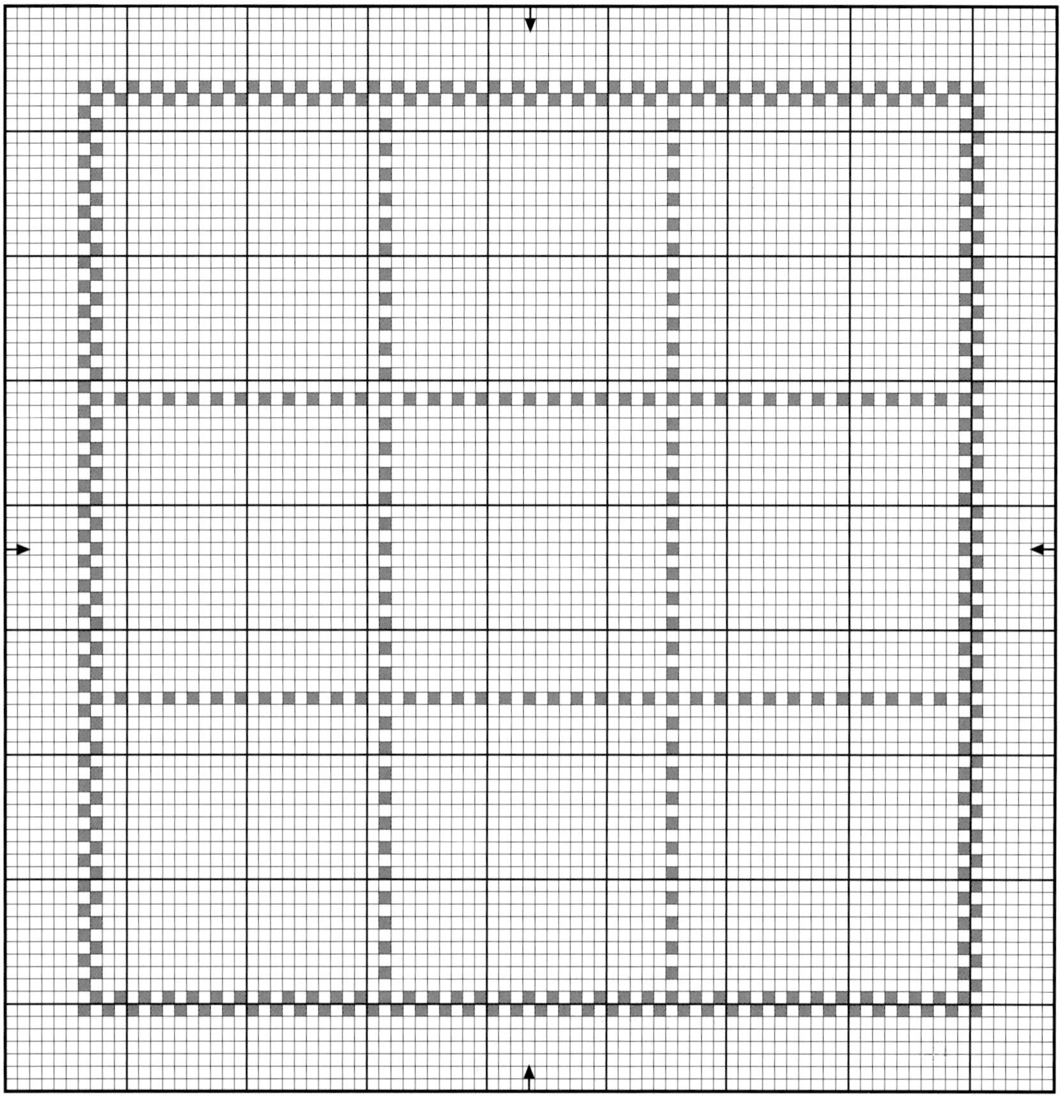

♥ Template 2 – Four Block Band

Used for the Four Seasons sampler on page 12
(Stitch count: 165h x 43w)

TOP

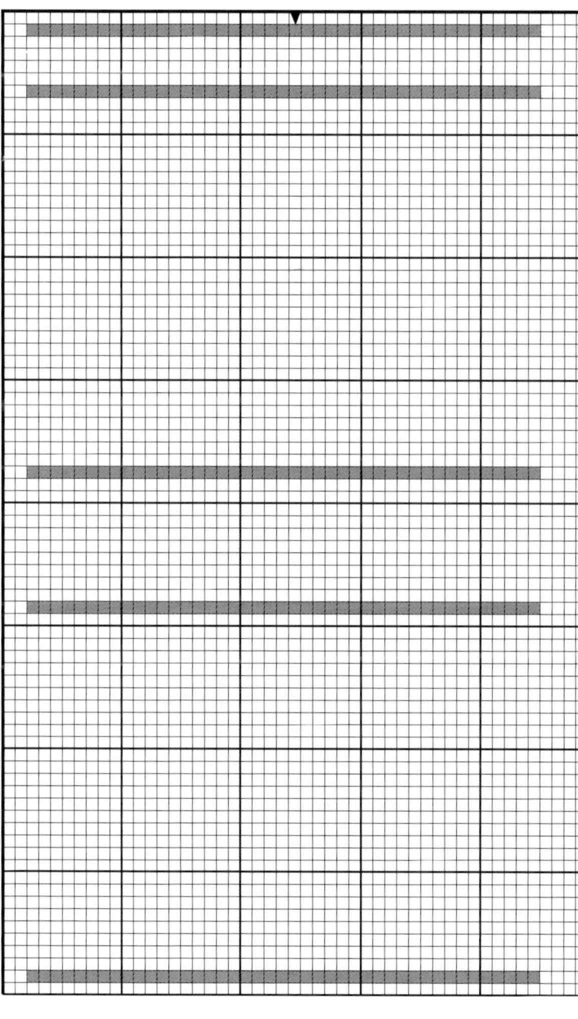

BOTTOM ← Join

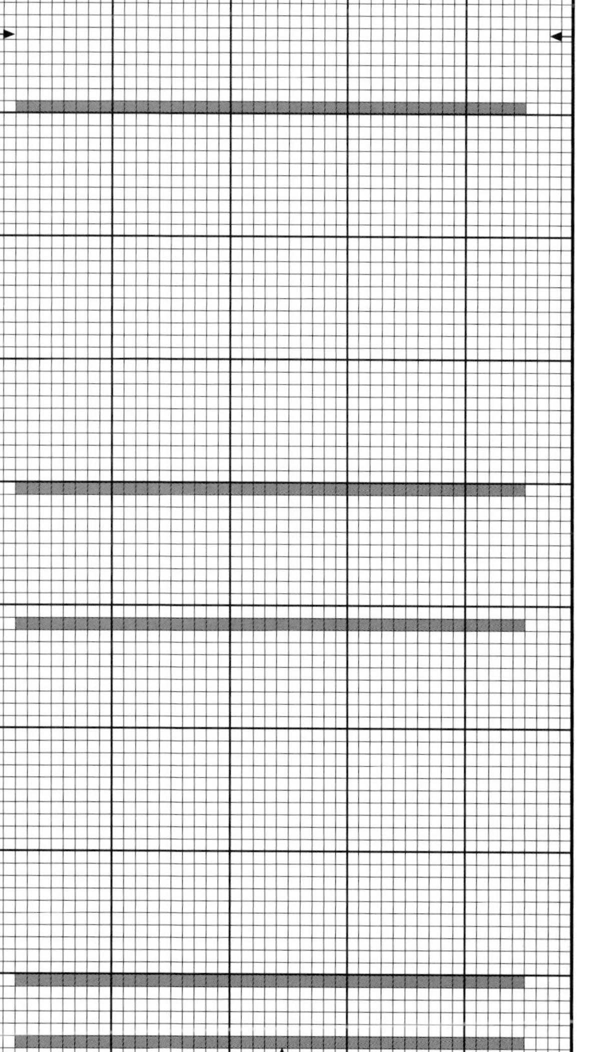

Template 3 – Traditional

Used for the Home and Garden sampler on page 16
(Stitch count: 110h x 89w)

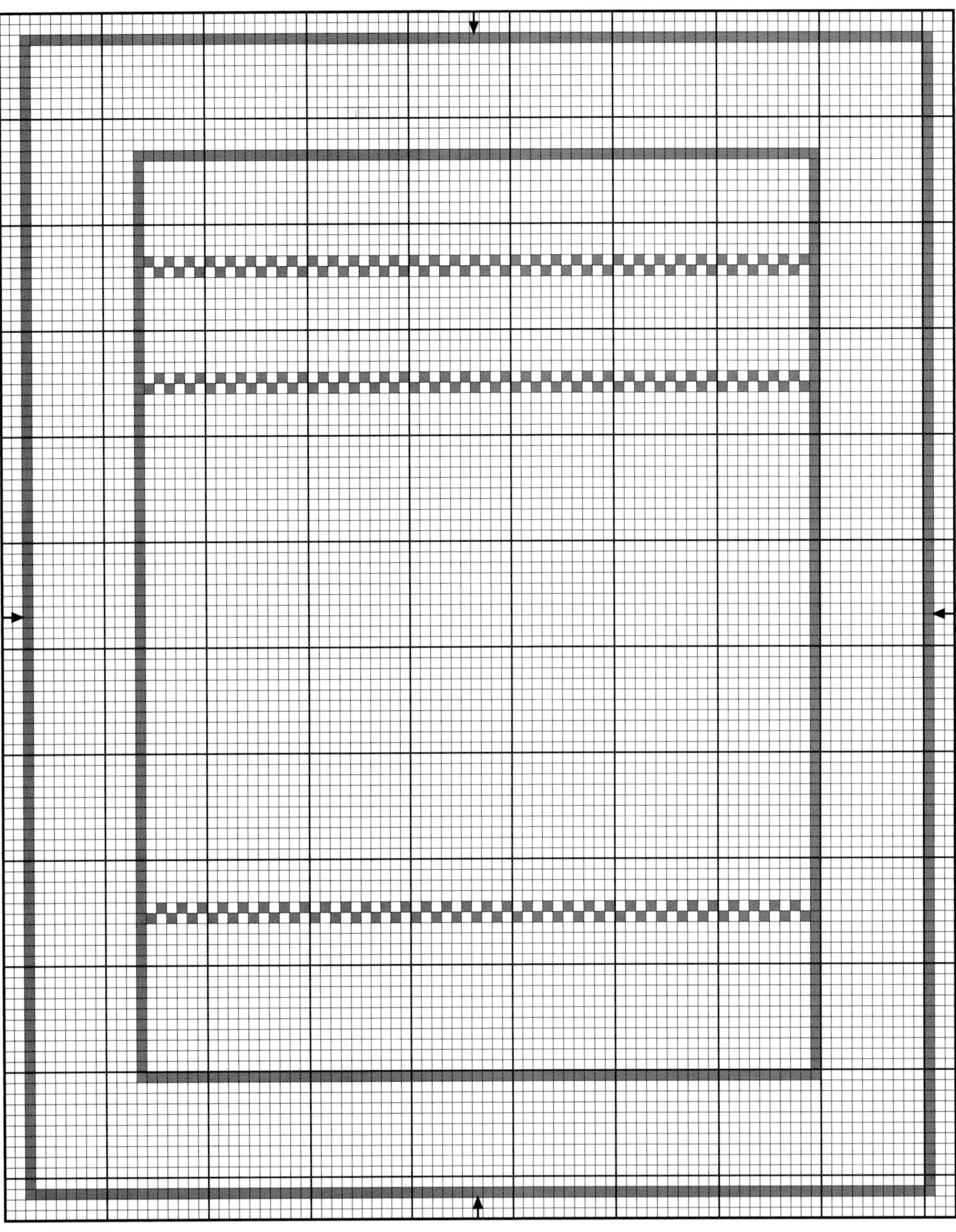

♥ Template 4 – Wide and Short

Used for the Welcome Baby sampler on page 18
(Stitch count: 134h x 95w)

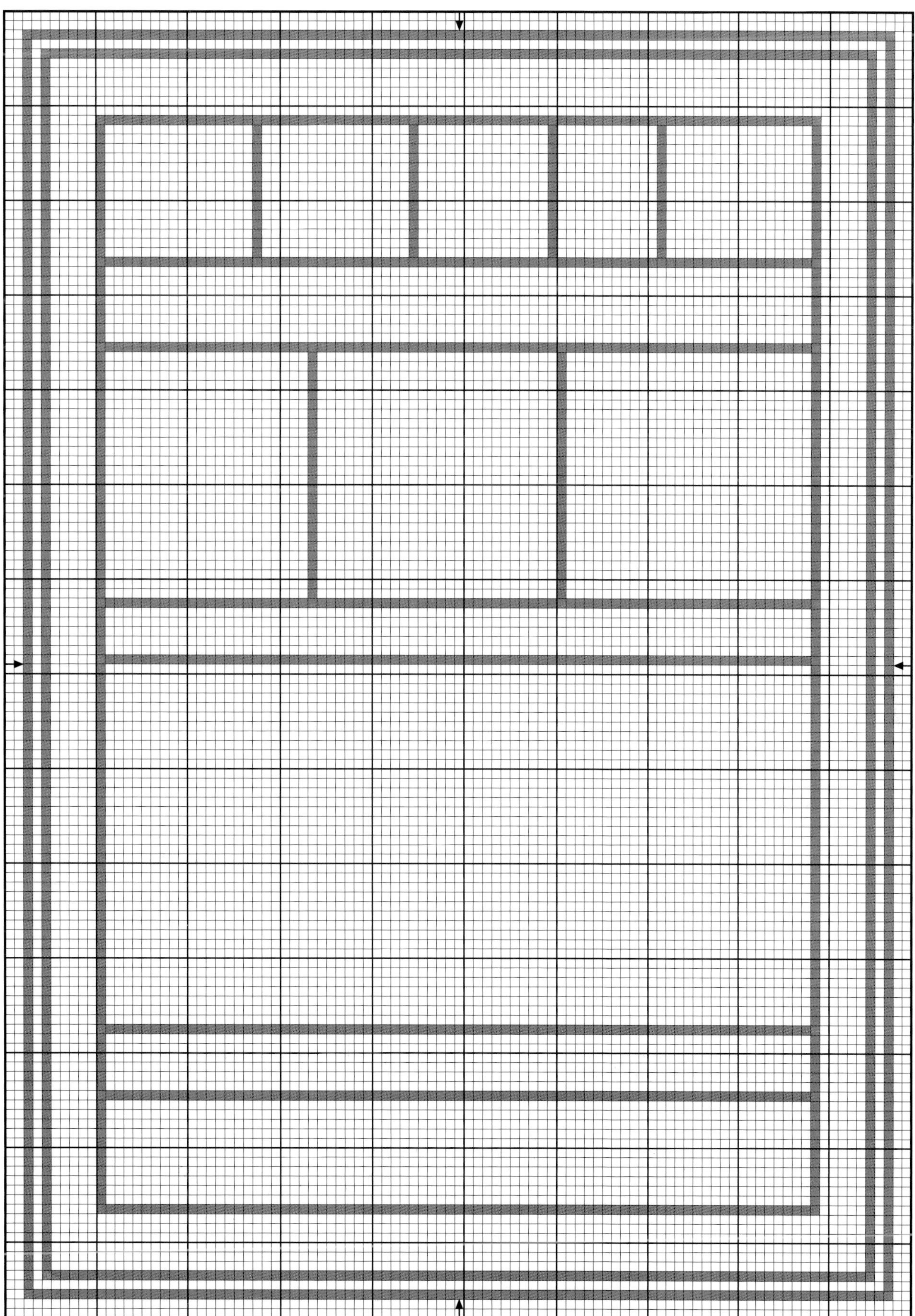

Sampler Templates

♥ Template 5 – Blocks in Band

Used for the Wedding Celebrations sampler on page 22 (Stitch count: 153h x 103w)

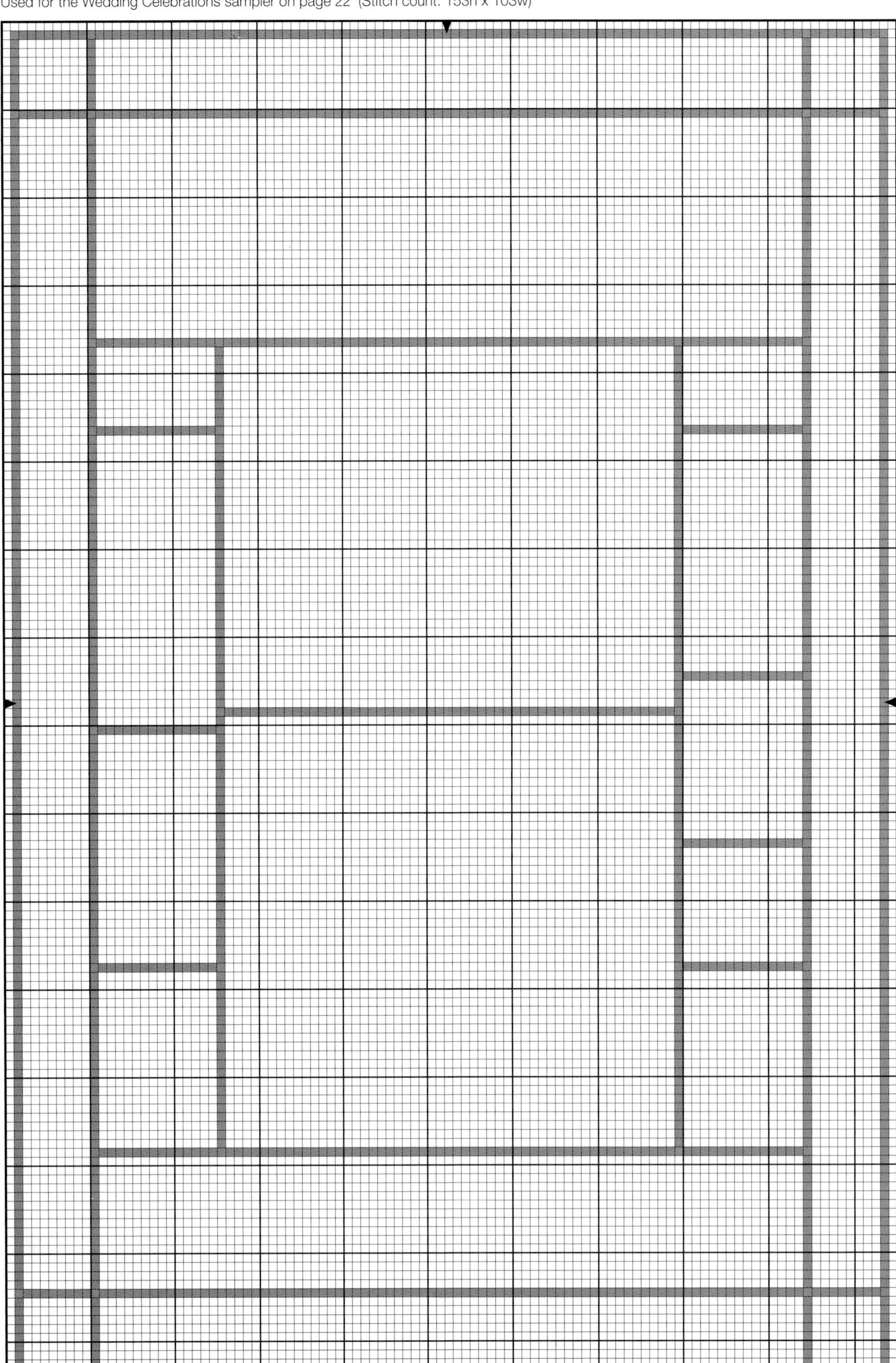

♥ Template 6 – Multi-Box

Used for the Very Merry Christmas sampler on page 24
(Stitch count: 104h x 85w)

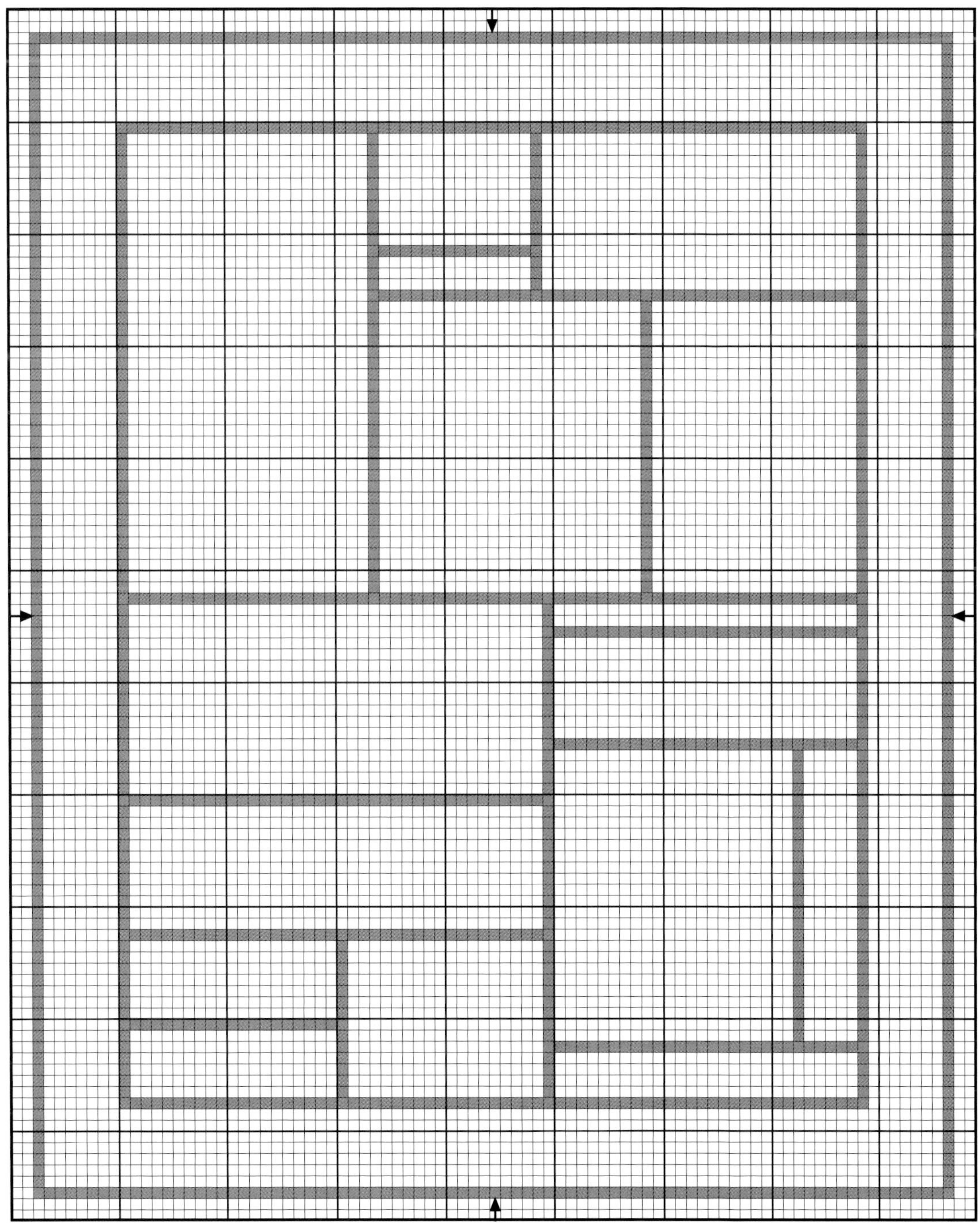

♥ Template 7 – Blocks in Long Band

Used for the Happy Families sampler on page 28 (join up the two chart parts)
(Stitch count: 185h x 101w)

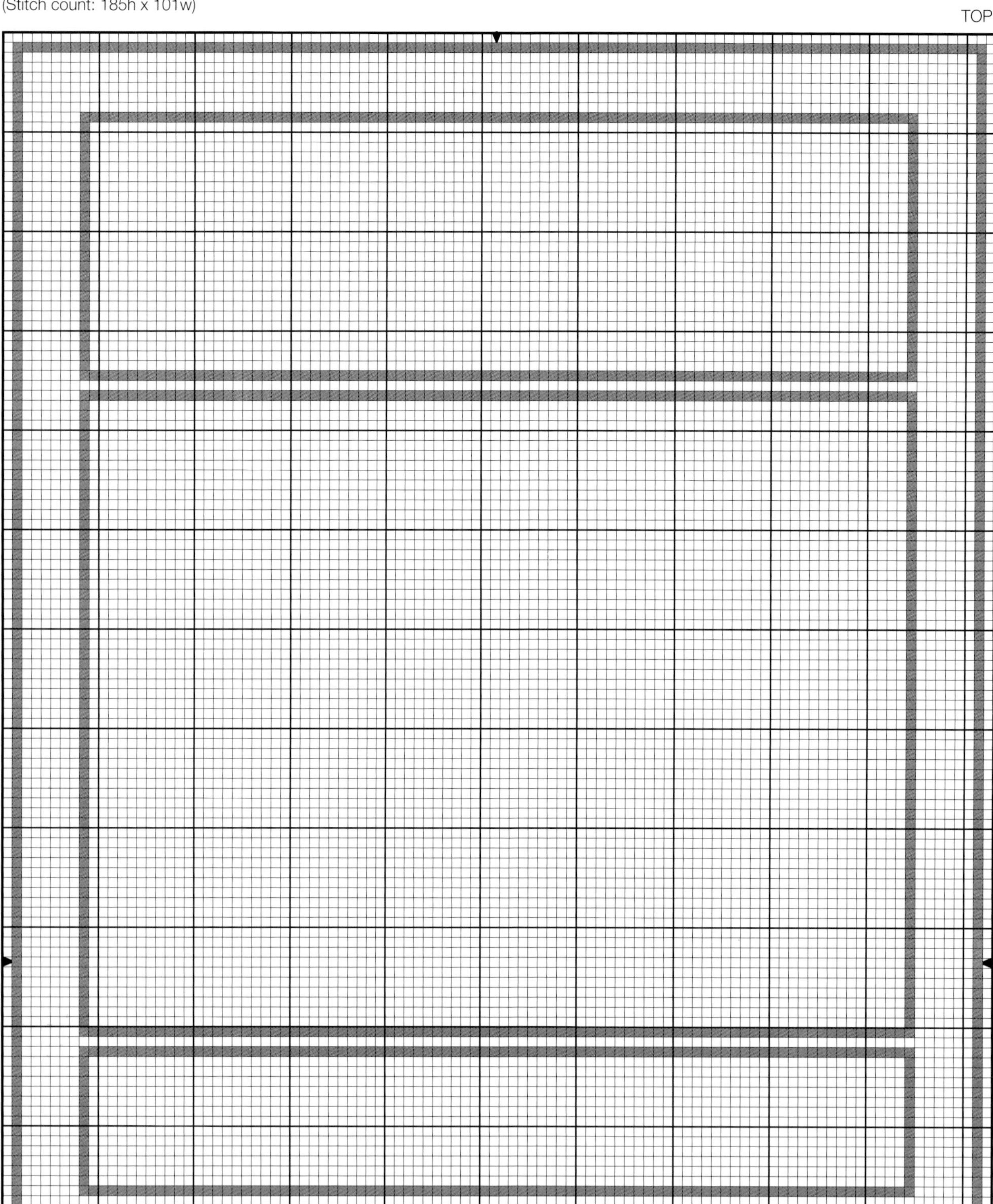

BOTTOM

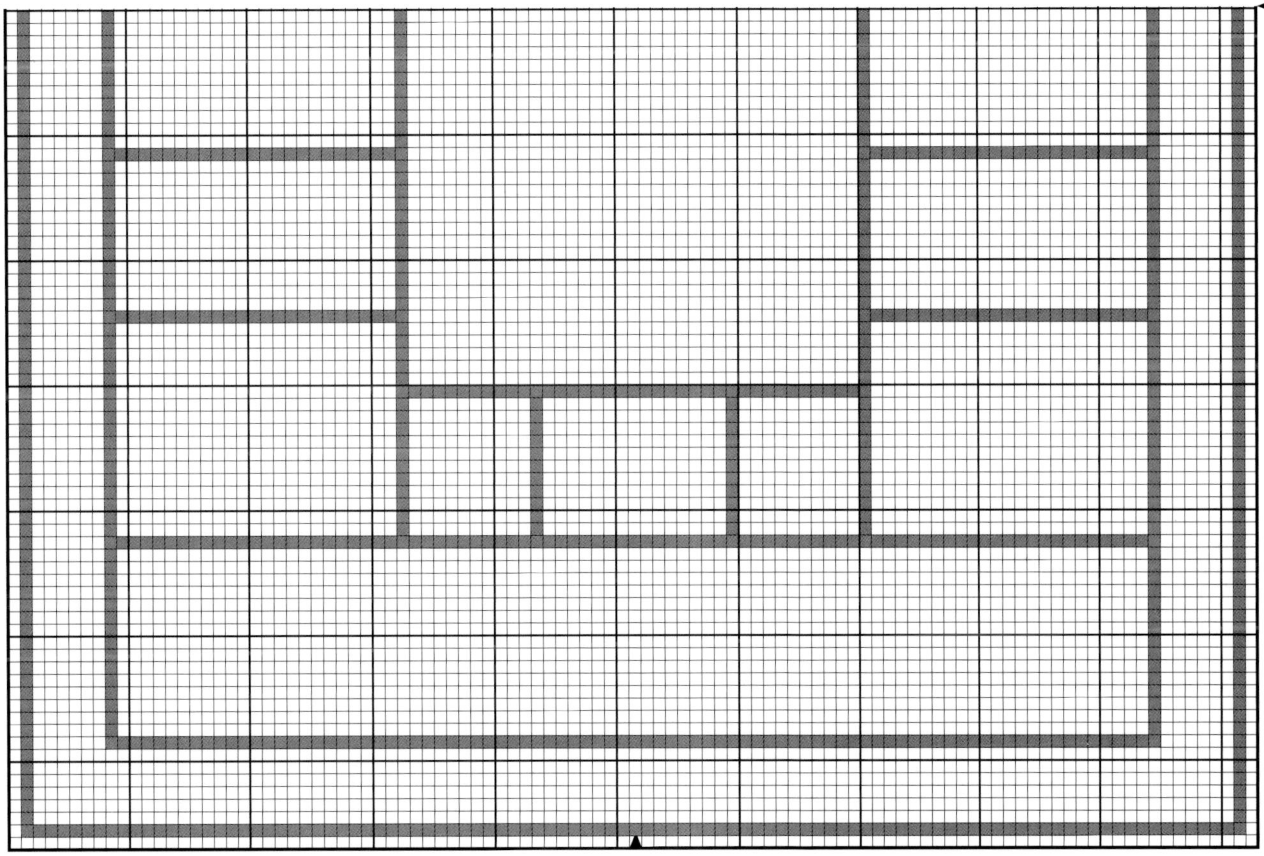

← Join

our
FAMILY
IS A CIRCLE OF LOVE
ABCDEFGHIJKL
MNOPQRSTUV
WXYZ123
POLLY JOHNSON JAMES BLAKE
WERE MARRIED 10 SEPTEMBER 1994
1995
JOSH
2000
SAM
1997
HARRIET
2003
ELLIE
PLUM TREE COTTAGE
Bless Our Family

MERRY
Christmas
PEACE AND JOY TO ALL
abcdefghijklm
nopqrstuvwx
yz123456
O LITTLE TOWN
OF BETHLEHEM

♥ Template 8 - Simple Adaptable

Used for the Holiday Memories sampler on page 32
(Stitch count: 121h x 72w)

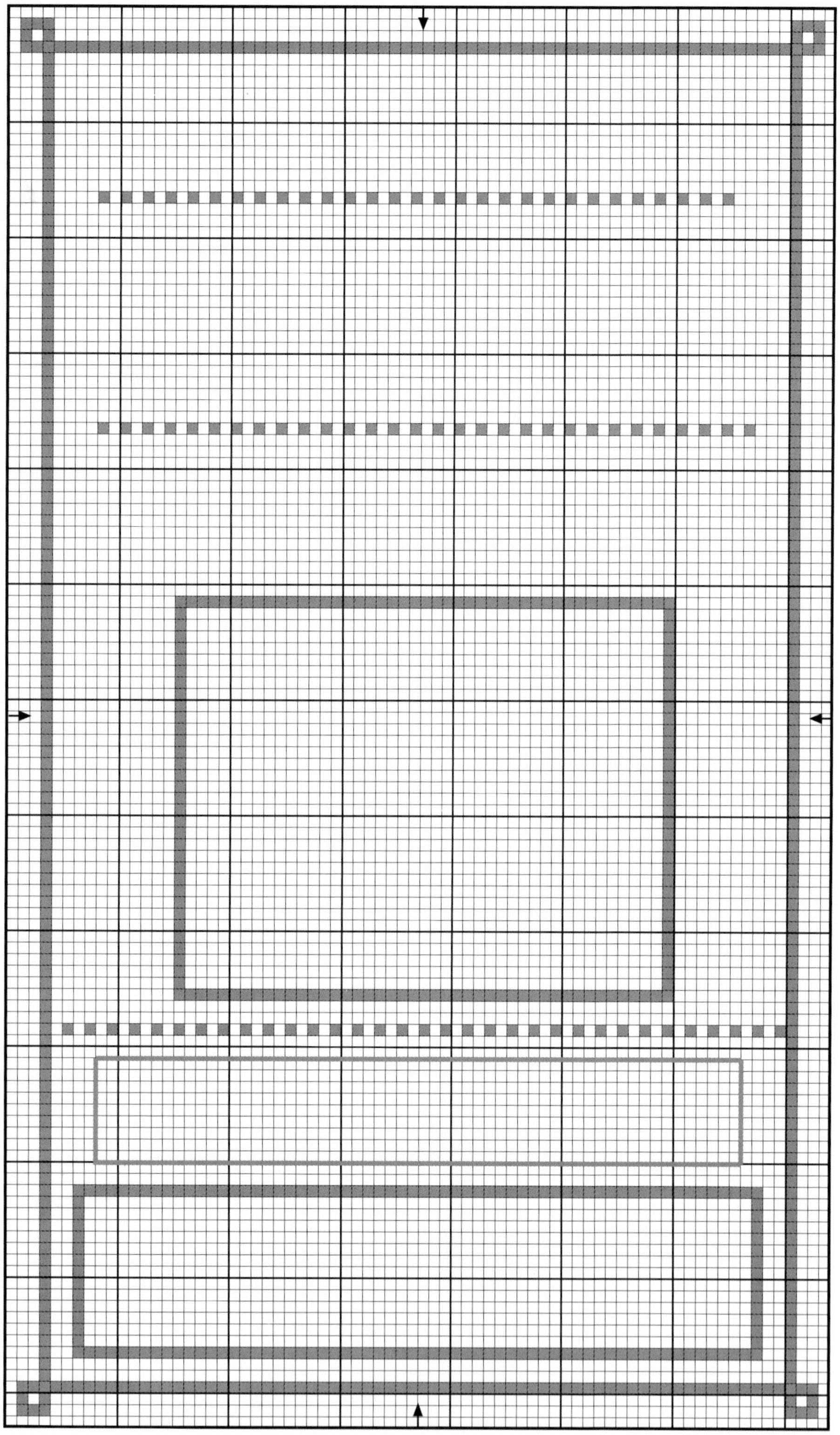

Techniques and Making Up

This section contains the basic techniques you will need to work any of the projects in the book and should be particularly useful to beginners.

Preparing the Fabric

It is a good idea before starting to stitch to check the design size given with each project and make sure that the embroidery fabric you plan to use is larger than this size. To allow for working and making up your fabric should be about 5cm (2in) larger all the way round than the finished size of the stitching. It is also a good idea before beginning to stitch to neaten and protect the fabric edges, especially linen which frays easily, either by hemming, zigzag stitching or using masking tape which can be removed later.

Finding the centre of the fabric is necessary in order that the stitched design will be centred on the fabric. To find the centre, fold the fabric in half horizontally and then vertically. Mark the centre point where the two lines meet with a fabric marker or mark the folds with tailor's chalk. As you work, this point on the fabric should correspond to the centre point on the chart. Remove marks on completion of the work.

Using the Charts and Keys

Counted cross stitch charts are easy to work from: each square on the chart represents one stitch. Each coloured square or coloured square with a symbol represents a thread colour, with the code number given in the chart key. I've used DMC stranded cotton (floss) but ask at your needlecraft store for Anchor equivalents if required. Some of the designs use fractional stitches (three-quarter cross stitches) to give more detail to the design. Solid coloured lines show where to work backstitches or star stitches. French knots are shown by coloured circles. Larger coloured circles with a dot are beads. When stitching motifs from the Motif Library, only use only the key that appears with that chart page.

Each complete sampler design has arrows at the sides to indicate the centre point of the design and you could mark this point with a pen or pencil. For your own use, you could enlarge the charts by colour photocopying.

Working the Stitches

There are no complicated stitches to master: all of those used within the projects are described here with simple diagrams.

Starting and Finishing

It is always a good idea to start and finish work correctly, to create the neatest effect and avoid ugly bumps and threads trailing across the back of work.

To start off a length of thread, knot one end, then push the needle through to the back of the fabric, about 2.5cm (1in) from your intended starting point, leaving the knot on the right side (see Fig 1). Stitch towards the knot, securing the thread at the back of the fabric as you go. When the thread is secure, cut off the knot.

To finish off a thread or start new threads, simply weave the needle and thread into the back of several worked stitches and then trim off neatly.

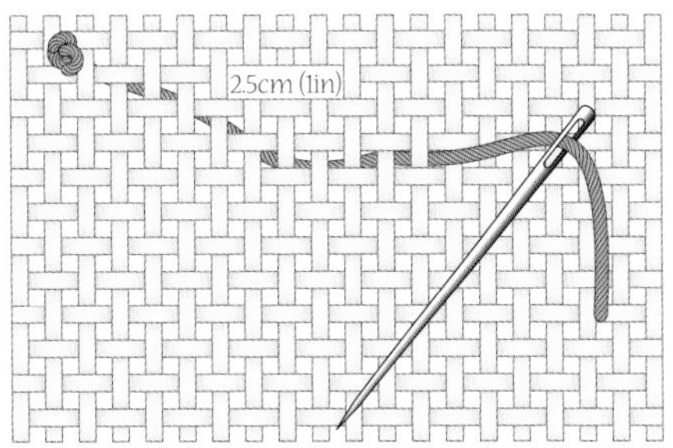

Fig 1 Beginning stitching neatly

Backstitching and Outlining

Backstitch is indicated on the charts by a solid coloured line. It can be worked on its own for lettering, on top of other stitches for detail and as an outline around areas of cross stitches to add definition. Most backstitch is worked with one strand of thread.

To work backstitch, bring the needle up through the fabric at 1 (Fig 2), then take it down at 2. Bring it back up at 3 and then down at 1. Repeat the process to make the next stitch.

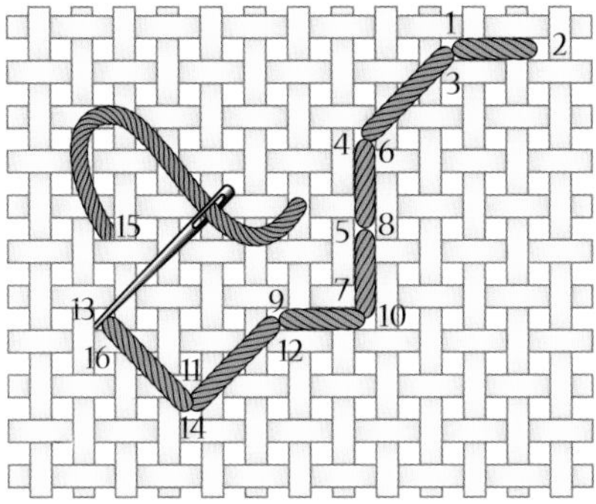

Fig 2 Backstitch

Cross Stitch

This is the main stitch used throughout the projects and each complete cross stitch is represented on the charts by a coloured square. The cross stitches in this book are worked over two threads of evenweave (linen) or one block of blockweave (Aida).

Fig 3 A single cross stitch on Aida

A cross stitch is worked in two stages: a diagonal stitch is worked over two threads (or one block), then a second diagonal stitch is worked over the first stitch in the opposite direction, forming a cross (see Fig 3). To stitch a large area you could work cross stitches in rows. Work a row of half cross stitches in one direction, then work back in the opposite direction with diagonal stitches to complete each cross stitch (Fig 4). The upper stitches of the crosses should lie in the same direction to produce a neat effect.

Fig 4 Cross stitch in rows

French Knot

This is a useful little stitch and is used in addition to cross stitch to add texture and emphasis. In this book they are worked with one or two strands of thread and are shown on the charts by a small coloured circle.

To work a French knot, bring the needle up to the right side of the fabric, hold the thread down with your left thumb (if right-handed) and wind the thread around the needle twice. Still holding the thread taut, put the needle through to the back of the work, one thread or part of a block away from the entry point (Fig 5). If you want bigger knots, add more thread to the needle.

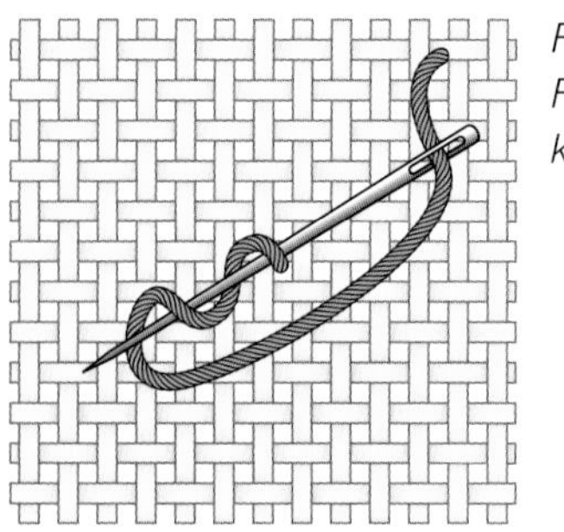

Fig 5a French knot

Fig 5b

Star Stitch

This stitch has been worked on some of the samplers and cards to create simple stars. Follow Fig 6, working in the same direction around each stitch, always passing the needle down through the central hole. You can vary the lengths of the 'arms' to create different shaped stars (Fig 7).

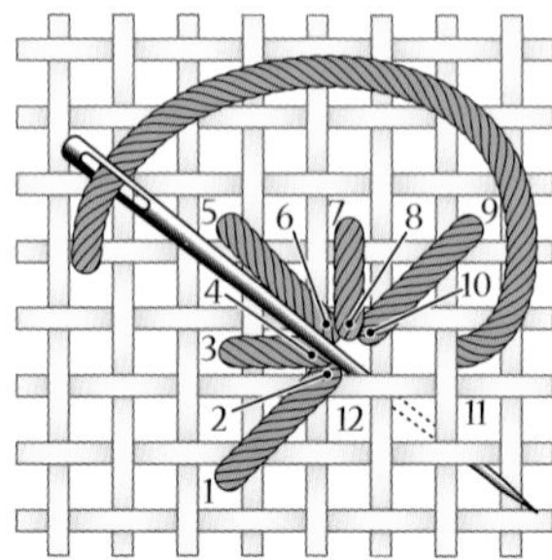

Fig 6 Working star stitch

Fig 7 Star stitch variation

Three-quarter Cross Stitch

This is a part or fractional stitch that is useful for adding detail to a design and creating smoother curves or circles. Three-quarter cross stitch is shown on the charts by a coloured triangle within a square.

To work three-quarter cross stitch, work a half cross stitch, then add a quarter stitch in the opposite direction, bringing the needle down in the centre of the half cross stitch already worked (Fig 8).

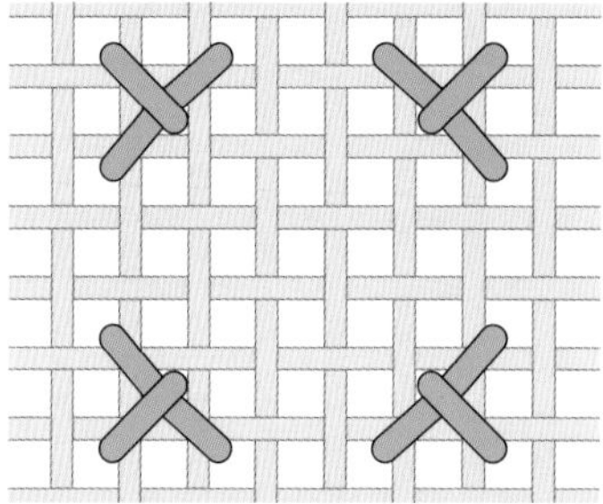

Fig 8 Three-quarter cross stitch

Caring for Finished Work

Cross stitch embroidery can be washed and ironed, though care should be taken with delicate ceramic buttons. Make sure it is colourfast first, then wash with bleach-free soap in hand-hot water, squeezing gently but never rubbing or wringing. Rinse in plenty of cold or lukewarm water and dry naturally.

To iron cross stitch embroidery, use a hot setting on a steam iron. Cover the ironing board with a thick layer of towelling and place the stitching on this, right side down. Press the fabric firmly but avoid any charms, buttons or metallic threads used.

Mounting and Framing

It really is best to take large samplers and pictures to a professional framer, where you will be able to choose from a wide variety of mounts and frames which will best enhance your work. The framer will be able to lace and stretch the fabric correctly and cut any surrounding mounts accurately. Embroideries with three-dimensional embellishments, such as shells or medals, are best framed without glass.

If mounting work into commercial products, such as box lids, follow the manufacturer's instructions. For small pieces of work, back with lightweight iron-on interfacing to stop the fabric wrinkling, and then mount.

If you intend to mount the work yourself, use acid-free mounting board in a colour that won't show through the embroidery. Cut the board to fit inside your picture frame and allow for the thickness of the fabric pulled over the edges of the board. There are two common methods used for mounting – taping and lacing

Taping Method

Place the cut board on the back of the work in the position required. Starting from the centre of one of the longest edges, fold the fabric firmly over the board and then pin through the fabric into the edge of the board to keep the fabric from moving. Check it is in the correct place with no wrinkles or bumps, then stick the work in place using strips of double-sided adhesive tape, removing the pins once finished (Fig 9).

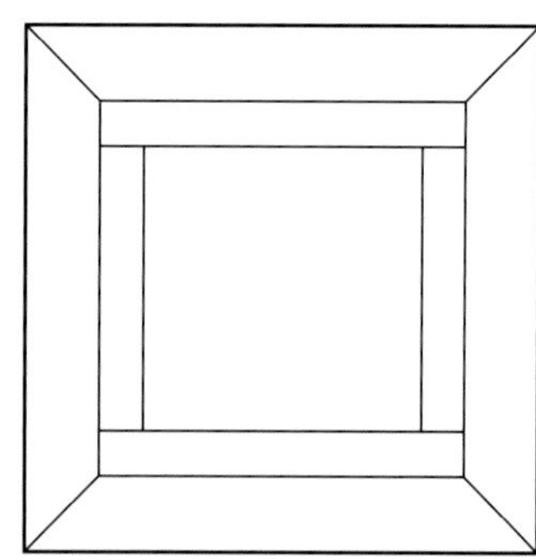

Fig 9 Taping method

Lacing Method

Pin the work in place on the board, as above, then working from the centre and using long lengths of very strong thread, lace backwards and forwards across the gap (Fig 10). Repeat this process for the shorter sides, taking care to mitre or fold the corners in neatly. Remove the pins once finished.

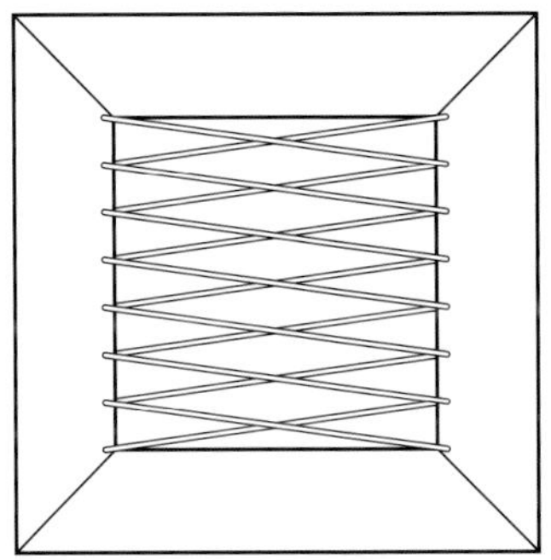

Fig 10 Lacing method

Mounting Work into Ready-made Items

There are many ready-made items specially made for displaying embroidery, including notebooks, coasters, rulers, pen holders, fridge magnets, key rings, name plates and bibs. Mount your work into these items following the manufacturer's instructions. Use a piece of paper or thin card to hide the back of any stitching that may be seen. It also helps to back the stitched design with iron-on interfacing to add stiffness and prevent fabric fraying.

Mounting Work into Cards

There are many lovely card mounts available today. They usually come pre-folded with three sections, the middle one having a window for your embroidery.

First make sure your embroidery looks good in the window space, then trim your design to the correct size to fit. Position small lengths of double-sided adhesive tape around the window area then remove the backing from the tape. Lay the card on top of the embroidery so that it shows neatly through the window and press into place. Fold the third of the card to cover the back of the embroidery, ensuring that the card opens correctly before securing with more double-sided tape (Fig 11).

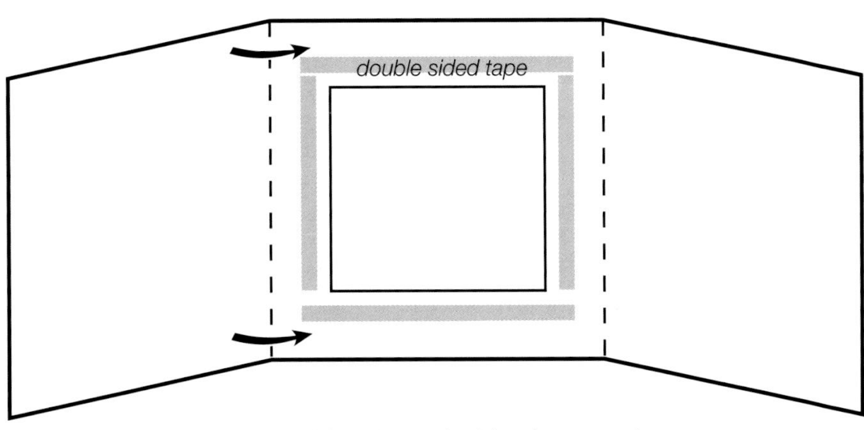

Fig 11 Mounting embroidery into a card

Making up a Pillow

The ring pillow on page 22 is easy to make and the instructions could be used for other cushions and scented sachets. Its finished size is about 16.5 x 15cm (7 x 6in).

When stitching is complete, trim the linen to about 20.5 x 18cm (8 x 7in). Sew on two pieces of narrow organza ribbon for the wedding rings to be tied to (see photo below for positions). Take a second piece of linen the same size and match it right sides together with the embroidered piece. Trim edges if necessary and insert a length of white lace into the seam all the way round. Sew round three sides, turn the pillow right way out, stuff firmly with polyester stuffing then sew up the fourth side, catching the lace in the seam as you do so.

Making up a Tree Decoration

This sweet little hanging from page 24 has a finished size of about 6 x 10cm (2½ x 4in).

When stitching is complete, trim the linen to about 10 x 12.5cm (4 x 5in). Take a second piece of linen the same size and place right sides together with the embroidered piece. Sew round three sides, inserting a length of ribbon in the top seam for a hanging loop. Turn the decoration to the right side, stuff with polyester stuffing and sew up the last side. Stitch twisted cord around the outside of the decoration.

Suppliers

UK

The American Way
30 Edgbaston Road, Smethwick,
West Midlands B66 4LQ
tel: 0121 601 5454
For Mill Hill buttons, charms, wire hangers and many other supplies

Coats Crafts UK
PO Box 22, Lingfield Estate, McMullen Road,
Darlington, County Durham DL1 1YQ
tel: +44 (0) 1325 365457 (for a list of stockists)
fax: +44 (0) 1325 338822
For Anchor stranded cotton (floss) and other embroidery supplies.

Craft Creations Limited
1C Ingersoll House, Delamare Road,
Cheshunt, Herts EN8 9HD
tel: 019992 781900
www.craftcreations.com
For greetings card blanks and card accessories

Dee Fine Arts
182 Telegraph Road, Heswall, Wirral CH60 0AJ
tel: 0151 3426657
For expert embroidery and picture framing

DMC Creative World
Pullman Road, Wigston,
Leicestershire LE18 2DY
tel: 0116 281 1040 fax: 0116 281 3592
www.dmc/cw.com
For threads and embroidery supplies

Forever England
No.6 The Old Yarn Mills, Westbury,
Sherborne, Dorset DT9 3RQ
tel: 01935 811970

Framecraft Miniatures Ltd
Unit 3, Isis House, Lindon Road, Brownhills,
West Midlands WS8 7BW
tel/fax (UK): 01543 360842
tel (international): 44 1543 453154
email: sales@framecraft.com
www.framecraft.com
For Mill Hill buttons, charms and many ready-made items including trinket bowls and boxes, notebook covers, pincushions and coasters

From Debbie Cripps
31 Lower Whitelands, Radstock, Bath BA3 3JW
www.debbiecripps.co.uk
For buttons, charms and embroidery supplies

Gregory Knopp
www.gregory-knopp.co.uk
For all kinds of folk-art buttons and embellishments

John Lewis
(Branches in many UK towns and cities)
For general haberdashery, decorated ribbons, felt, trimmings and embroidery supplies

Madeira Threads (UK) Ltd
PO Box 6, Thirsk, North Yorkshire YO7 3YX
tel: 01845 524880
email: info@madeira.co.uk
www.madeira.co.uk
For Madeira stranded cotton (floss) and other embroidery supplies

Merry Heart Designs
www.merryheart.co.uk
For cross stitch charts and books by Helen Philipps

Willow Fabrics
27 Willow Green, Knutsford WA16 6AX
tel: 0156562 1098
fax: 01565 653233
For linen, evenweave and Aida fabrics, stitching paper and many other needlework supplies

Voirrey Embroidery Centre
Brimstage Hall, Wirral CH63 6JA
tel: 0151 342 3514
fax: 0151 342 5161
For embroidery supplies, books and exhibitions

USA

The DMC Corporation
10 Port Kearney, South Kearney, NJ 070732
tel: 979 589 0606
www.dmc-usa.com
For DMC threads and fabrics and a wide range of needlework supplies

Mill Hill, a division of Wichelt Imports Inc.
N162 Hwy 35, Stoddard WI 54658
tel: 608 788 4600
fax: 608 788 6040
email: millhill@millhill.com
www. millhill.com
For Mill Hill beads and a US source for Framecraft products

Yarn Tree Designs
PO Box 724, Ames, Iowa 500100724
tel: 1 800 247 3952
www.yarntree.com
For cross stitch supplies and card mounts

Zweigart/Joan Toggit Ltd
262 Old Brunswick Road, Suite E, Piscataway,
NJ 08854-3756
tel: 732 562 8888
email: info@zweigart.com
www.zweigart.com
For a large selection of cross stitch fabrics and pre-finished items for embroidery

Acknowledgments

Thank you to everyone at David & Charles – to Cheryl Brown for commissioning this book and for her creative energy and ideas, to Prudence Rogers for her inspired book design, and to Lin Clements for her wonderful attention to detail when editing both text and charts. Thanks also to Jennifer Proverbs for all her hard work. Thanks to Kim Sayer for the beautiful photography. Thank you to DMC for supplying me with all the beautiful threads I need, and to The American Way for the buttons. Finally, a special thank you to my wonderful husband David and daughters Sarah and Rosie for all their support and encouragement.

About the Author

Helen Philipps studied printed textiles and embroidery at Manchester Metropolitan University and then taught drawing and design before becoming a freelance designer. After working in the greetings card industry, Helen's love of needlecraft led to her creating original designs for stitching magazines and her work is still featured regularly in *Cross Stitch Collection*, *Cross Stitcher* and *World of Cross Stitching*. In 2000 she set up Merry Heart Designs which specializes in bright, modern cross stitch charts. This is Helen's fourth book to be published by David & Charles.

Index

♥ Graph Paper

Use to make your own personal sampler, see pages 5–7

Andy.
07964 543461